Let Freedom Ring

The Plymouth Colony

by Pamela Dell

Consultant:
Marsha Hamilton
Assistant Professor of History
University of South Alabama
Mobile, Alabama

Capstone
press

Mankato, Minn

Capstone Press
151 Good Counsel Drive, P.O. Box 669, Mankato, Minnesota 56002
www.capstonepub.com

Books published by Capstone Press are manufactured with paper containing at least 10 percent post-consumer waste.

Library of Congress Cataloging-in-Publication Data
Dell, Pamela.
    The Plymouth Colony / by Pamela Dell.
    p. cm.—(Let freedom ring)
    Summary: Follows the struggles and triumphs of the colonists who came to the New World and founded Plymouth Colony in what would become Massachusetts.
    Includes bibliographical references (p. 45) and index.
    ISBN-13: 978-0-7368-2463-7 (hardcover)
    ISBN-10: 0-7368-2463-4 (hardcover)
    ISBN-13: 978-0-7368-4480-2 (softcover pbk.)
    ISBN-10: 0-7368-4480-5 (softcover pbk.)
    1. Massachusetts—History—New Plymouth, 1620–1691—Juvenile literature. 2. Pilgrims (New Plymouth Colony)—Juvenile literature. [1. Massachusetts—History—New Plymouth, 1620–1691. 2. Pilgrims (New Plymouth Colony)] I. Title. II. Series.
F68.D45 2004
974.4'02—dc22
                                          2003012136

Editorial Credits

Katy Kudela, editor; Kia Adams, series designer; Molly Nei, book designer and illustrator; Scott Thoms, photo researcher; Eric Kudalis, product planning editor

Photo Credits

Cover image: Painting of Pilgrims landing at Plymouth by Currier and Ives, Getty Images/Hulton Archive

Corbis, 15, 21, 27, 42; Bettmann, 5, 12, 32, 38, 43; Lake County Museum, 29
Getty Images/Hulton Archive, 7, 31, 37
The Granger Collection, New York, 19, 23, 24, 25, 30
Houserstock/Dave G. Houser, 41
North Wind Picture Archives, 10, 35
Courtesy of Pilgrim Hall Museum, Plymouth, Massachusetts, 9
Photri-Microstock, 13

Printed in the United States of America in Stevens Point, Wisconsin.
082010
005926R

Table of Contents

1   Land, Ahoy!   4

2   Finding Common Ground   8

3   A Hard Winter   14

4   Peace with American Indians   20

5   Alone in a New Land   28

6   Struggling to Survive   36

Features

Map: Plymouth Colony, 1620s   17

Time Line   42

Glossary   44

Read More   45

Useful Addresses   46

Internet Sites   47

Index   48

Chapter One

Land, Ahoy!

In November 1620, the passengers on board the *Mayflower* sighted land. The land was Cape Cod, in what is now the state of Massachusetts. Cape Cod was a welcome sight for the men, women, and children on board.

The *Mayflower*'s passengers set sail from England in September 1620. During the voyage, they braved the harsh waters of the Atlantic Ocean. They faced violent storms and damage to their ship. Many passengers suffered from seasickness.

The passengers' faith and courage kept them from turning back. They wanted to start a new life. Some were looking for religious freedom. Others were hoping to find riches.

The *Mayflower*'s journey across the Atlantic Ocean took at least 60 days.

The Pilgrims

Two groups of people sailed together on the *Mayflower*. These groups were known as the "Separatists" and the "Strangers."

Early in the 1600s, King James I of England announced his religious views. Anyone who did not worship in the Church of England could be punished. The Separatists wanted to separate themselves from the Church of England.

Fearing for their lives, many Separatists fled to Holland in 1608. The Separatists did not speak the Dutch language. Work was not easy to find. The Separatists set their hopes on present-day Virginia. A small group sailed from Holland back to England.

In London, the Separatists joined people eager to travel. The Separatists called this group "Strangers." Many of the Strangers were hoping to find riches. Most of the Strangers did not share the Separatists' religious views. They did share the hope of a better life elsewhere. Together these travelers became known as the **Pilgrims**.

In August 1620, the Pilgrims left England on board the *Mayflower* and the *Speedwell*. But the

Speedwell ran into trouble. The ships returned to England. After a second failed attempt to sail, the *Speedwell* was declared unsafe for the journey. Some of the *Speedwell*'s passengers decided not to travel. Others joined the passengers on the *Mayflower*. The *Mayflower* set sail a third time. This time the *Mayflower* sailed alone.

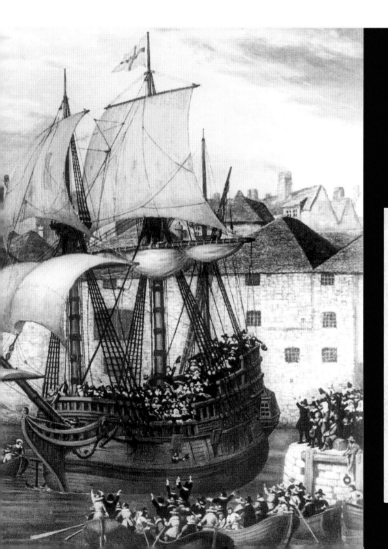

The *Mayflower* set sail from England in September 1620. To reach present-day America, the ship traveled 2,900 miles (4,667 kilometers).

Chapter Two

Finding Common Ground

In its voyage to North America, the *Mayflower* went badly off course. The Pilgrims had planned to settle in the area of present-day Virginia. As they sailed closer to shore in November 1620, the *Mayflower*'s passengers found they were well north of Virginia. The *Mayflower*'s captain tried to sail the ship south toward present-day Virginia.

Cape Cod Instead of Virginia

Fierce tides and wild currents forced the *Mayflower* to turn back. The ship anchored in Cape Cod Bay. With winter coming, the passengers gave up hope of reaching Virginia.

The Pilgrims had hoped to reach new land in time to plant crops. They wanted a fall harvest to feed them through the winter season.

The Pilgrims reached land in November 1620. Henry A. Bacon's 1877 painting shows the Pilgrims stepping onto Plymouth Rock.

The Pilgrims did not succeed in their plan. By the time they reached Cape Cod, winter was already on its way. The view before them was cold and empty. From the ship, the land appeared full of hidden dangers.

The Pilgrims were tired and weakened from the long journey. After landing in Cape Cod Bay, they were faced with the decision of where to settle the colony.

Plymouth Colony, 1620s

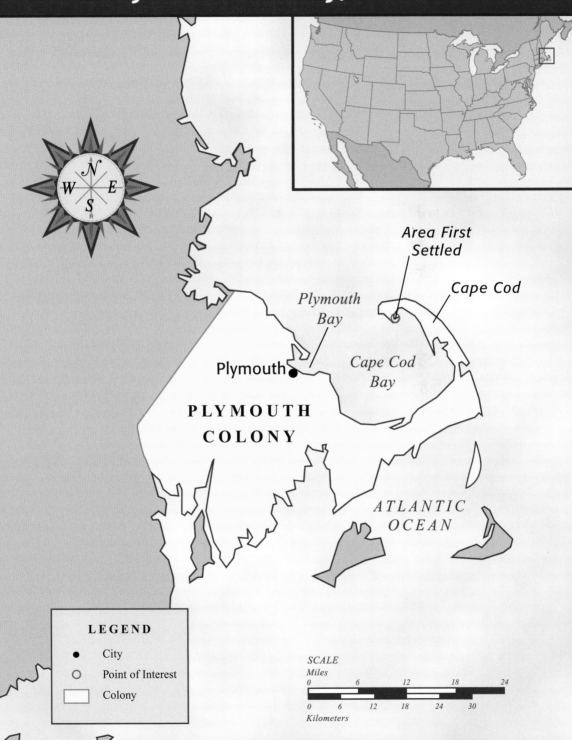

Area First Settled

Cape Cod

Plymouth Bay

Plymouth

Cape Cod Bay

PLYMOUTH COLONY

ATLANTIC OCEAN

LEGEND
- ● City
- ○ Point of Interest
- ▢ Colony

SCALE
Miles
0   6   12   18   24

0   6   12   18   24   30
Kilometers

The Great Sickness

During the first winter, many settlers became ill with **pneumonia**, a disease that infects the lungs. Others suffered from **scurvy**, a deadly disease that causes swollen limbs, bleeding gums, and weakness. By the end of February, only about 50 of the original 102 *Mayflower* passengers remained alive.

The Pilgrims first built a 20-foot (6-meter) long common house. This house provided shelter while they built individual family homes.

Building shelters was only one of many struggles the Pilgrims faced. Diseases quickly began to sweep through the colony. At times, only six or seven Pilgrims remained healthy. These settlers had to care for those that were ill.

Sickness continued to spread during January and February of 1621. The Pilgrims called this time the "Great Sickness." People were dying almost every day. At night, the bodies were buried in

Squanto and the Pilgrims

Squanto spoke English well. He helped the Pilgrims talk with other American Indians. He also taught the Pilgrims many important skills.

Squanto shared his knowledge of farming and hunting. He also taught the Pilgrims fishing skills.

Squanto shared his farming skills with the Pilgrims. He also taught the Pilgrims how to fish and hunt on the land.

The Pilgrims learned the best ways to catch fish. They also learned to tell when the fish swam down the streams. Squanto soon became an important part of Plymouth Colony.

Chief Massasoit wished to create peace with the Pilgrims. He traveled with Samoset and Squanto to Plymouth Colony.

Many people visit Plimoth Plantation in Plymouth, Massachusetts. The living history museum offers visitors a view of colonial life in 1627.

TIME LINE

September—The *Mayflower* leaves for North America.

November—The *Mayflower* drops anchor in Cape Cod Bay.

March—Samoset speaks with the Pilgrims; Pilgrims create a peace treaty with Wampanoag.

A group of Separatists emigrate to Holland.

1608   **1620**   **1621**

October—The Pilgrims celebrate their first harvest Thanksgiving in Plymouth.

December—Pilgrims anchor ship in Plymouth Bay.

Late December—Pilgrims begin building their colony.

William Bradford dies from an illness; he served as Plymouth's governor for 36 years.

Plymouth Colony becomes part of the Massachusetts Bay Colony.

| 1648 | 1657 | 1661 | 1691 |

Chief Massasoit dies; the Pilgrims begin to have increased troubles with the Wampanoag and other American Indians.

The colonists pay their debt in full to the merchant adventurers in London.

Glossary

colonist (KOL-uh-nist)—person who makes a home in a new area

grant (GRANT)—a gift such as land or money given for a particular purpose

Pilgrim (PIL-gruhm)—one of the English Separatists or Strangers who settled in North America in 1620

pneumonia (noo-MOH-nyuh)—a disease that causes the lungs to become infected and fill with liquid

Puritan (PYOOR-uh-tuhn)—one of a group of Protestants in the 1500s and 1600s who sought simple church services and a strict moral code; many Puritans fled England and settled in North America.

scurvy (SKUR-vee)—a deadly disease caused by lack of vitamin C; scurvy produces swollen limbs, bleeding gums, and weakness.

settlement (SET-uhl-muhnt)—a colony or group of people who have left one place to make a home in another place

survivor (sur-VYE-vur)—someone who lives through a disaster or horrible event

treaty (TREE-tee)—an official agreement between two or more groups or countries

Read More

Collier, Christopher, and James Lincoln Collier. *Pilgrims and Puritans: 1620–1676.* The Drama of American History. New York: Benchmark Books, 1998.

Grace, Catherine O'Neill, and Margaret M. Bruchac, with Plimoth Plantation. *1621: A New Look at Thanksgiving.* Washington, D.C.: National Geographic Society, 2001.

Santella, Andrew. *The Plymouth Colony.* We the People. Minneapolis: Compass Point Books, 2001.

Schmidt, Gary D. *William Bradford: Plymouth's Faithful Pilgrim.* Grand Rapids, Mich.: Eerdmans Books for Young Readers, 1999.

Witteman, Barbara. *Miles Standish: Colonial Leader.* Let Freedom Ring. Mankato, Minn.: Bridgestone Books, 2004.

Useful Addresses

Miles Standish Monument
Crescent Street
Duxbury, MA 02332
This monument in Duxbury was built in honor of Miles Standish, a military leader in Plymouth Colony.

National Monument to the Forefathers
Allerton Street
Plymouth, MA 02360
Built to honor Plymouth's founders, this monument in Plymouth is one of the largest statues in the United States. It stands 81 feet (25 meters) tall. The names of the *Mayflower*'s passengers are etched into the stone.

Pilgrim Hall Museum
75 Court Street
Plymouth, MA 02360
This museum houses the world's largest and most complete collection of Pilgrim artifacts.

Plimoth Plantation
137 Warren Avenue
P.O. Box 1620
Plymouth, MA 02362
This outdoor living history museum is built on the actual site of the original Plymouth Colony. Visitors to this museum can learn about life in Plymouth Colony in 1627.

Internet Sites

Facthound offers a safe, fun way to find Internet sites related to this book. All of the sites on Facthound have been researched by our staff.

Here's how:
1. Visit *www.facthound.com*
2. Type in this special code **0736824634** for age-appropriate sites.
   Or enter a search word related to this book for a more general search.
3. Click on the Fetch It button.

Facthound will fetch the best sites for you!

Index

Abenaki. See American Indians
American Indians, 14, 16, 19, 20, 23,
    28, 39
    Abenaki, 22
    Patuxet, 22, 25
    Wampanoag, 22, 25, 26, 27, 28, 34

Bradford, William, 12, 31, 33, 34, 35

Cape Cod, 4, 10, 15, 16
Cape Cod Bay, 8, 10, 14, 30
Carver, John, 13, 26, 27, 28, 32, 33
crops, 8, 16, 33

diseases, 18–19, 25, 28

expeditions, 14, 16

food, 14, 15, 20, 33, 34, 36, 37, 39
Fortune, 39

Great Sickness. See diseases

housing, 18, 20, 21

interpreter, 25, 26

James I (King of England), 6
James II (King of England), 40

land grant, 11

Massasoit, 24, 26, 27, 34

Mayflower, 4, 5, 6, 7, 8, 12, 14, 28, 39
    anchors in Plymouth, 16
    passengers on board, 4, 7, 8, 18
    returns to England, 28–30
    ship's crew, 28
Mayflower Compact, 12, 13
merchant adventurers, 11

Patuxet. See American Indians
peace treaty, 26, 27, 28
Plimoth Plantation, 40, 41
Plymouth Bay, 16
Plymouth Rock, 9
Puritans, 36

religion, 4, 6, 30, 39

Samoset, 22, 24, 26
Separatists, 6, 11, 12, 13, 31, 39
Speedwell, 6, 7
Squanto, 22, 23, 24, 25, 26
Standish, Miles, 12, 31
Strangers, 6, 11, 12

Thanksgiving, 33–34, 35
trading posts, 38
treaty. See peace treaty

Virginia, 6, 8

Wampanoag. See American Indians
Winslow, Edward, 35

KNITTED
TAMS

MARY ROWE

Interweave Press
Loveland, Colorado

All the tams in the photographs have been designed and knitted by Mary Rowe.
The following tams appear courtesy of their owners:

    "Firefly Fantasy," Cozy Baker
    "Plum Pizzicato," Pat Seamon
    star tam (page 9), Mary Bratz-Stephens
    "Woodland Fantasy," Magdalena McMillan
    "Sweet Melodies," Mary Bratz-Stephens
    "Jazzy Blues," June Rinck
    "Black Star Rising," Cozy Baker
    untitled (page 47), Margaret Hatton
    "Ruby Rondo," Alda Siegan
    "Amethyst Adagio," Cozy Baker

 Interweave Press, Inc.
201 East Fourth Street
Loveland, Colorado 80537-5655
www.interweave.com

LIBRARY OF CONGRESS CATALOGING-IN-PUBLICATION DATA
Rowe, Mary.
   Knitted tams/Mary Rowe.
      p.   cm.
   Bibliography: p.
   Includes index.
   ISBN 0-934026-48-3
    1.Knitting—Patterns. 2. Berets. I. Title.
TT825.R68 1989   89-7438
746.9'2-dc20   CIP

15 14 13 12 11 10 9 8 7

Dedication

. . .To Elizabeth Zimmermann for the inspiration to pursue my own creations in knitting.

. . .To Schätzi McMillan, my sister, for her long support of my craft and her wonderment at my creations. She was the first to suggest that these tam-o'-shanters were a special kind of art.

. . .To my first knitting teacher, Dode Rubison, for sharing her skill with patience, kindness, and love.

Contents

Acknowledgments

Part 1 Tam Beginnings 1
Introduction: The story of my fascination with tams 1
A short history of tams 2
The idea of the tam 6
Materials 7
Techniques 11
Abbreviations 17

Part 2 Tam Basics 19
The basic 10-inch tam 19
Adding color patterns to the basic tam 22

Part 3 Special Sizing for Basic Tams 25
Changing the head size 25
Changing the finished diameter of the tam:
    getting ready 26
Changing the finished diameter of the tam:
    making the adjustments 30

Part 4 Wheel Patterns for the Basic Tam 35
Using the basic pattern graph 36
Designing shapes 36
More elaborate patterns 42

Part 5 Color 44
Using color 44
Color in Fair Isle patterns 45
My favorite color combinations 46

Part 6 Variations   52
    Top decrease variations and finishing options
      for the basic tam   53
    Shaping variations and additional sizing information
      for the basic tam   57
    Garland patterns and yoke-type decreasing   70
    Wall tams   72
    Tam mastery   76

Part 7 Summary   77
    The essential tam   77
    Tam worksheet   78

Afterword   83

Appendix   84
    Border patterns   84
    Wheel patterns   91
    Color numbers for Shetland yarn   96
    Source list   98

Bibliography   100

Index   103

Acknowledgments

Special thanks to Meg Swansen. Her kindness and generosity in sharing expertise, encouragement, and friendship have helped me through some difficult times both with this book and in my personal life. Her assistance with the manuscript and last-minute additions and corrections have been invaluable. Thank you, Meg, for giving me courage and persistence.

Thank you to Marianne for the gift of the Zaninni photo collection, to Ruth Melville and Lizbeth Upitis for their comments and editorial assistance, and finally to my knitting class at the Lincoln Center, Portage County Commission on Aging, Stevens Point, Wisconsin, who helped to prove the basic pattern in several weights and types of yarn.

PART 1
Tam Beginnings

INTRODUCTION
THE STORY OF MY FASCINATION WITH TAMS

Long before I began knitting I was fascinated by the use of round shapes in the fine and applied arts. I collected pictures of mandalas, plates, clocks, Aztec and Mayan calendars, and unusually shaped illuminated manuscripts. As I progressed in knitting I became interested in producing circular (not tubular) shapes...a difficult task if one considers only sweaters.

As I read, studied, and knitted I began to collect information on the use of circular motifs in knitting. In Victorian times, they appeared in lace tablecloths and at the backs of baby bonnets. Still, these lace motifs did not satisfy my desire to experiment with color.

I abandoned my search for circular color motifs in knitting and centered my study on the lovely Fair Isle color patterns of the Shetland Islands. I was delighted to discover the circular color motifs on the back of Sheila McGregor's *The Complete Book of Traditional Fair Isle Knitting*. However, the book contained only a few sentences on the construction of these motifs.

Another inspiration came from Elizabeth Zimmermann. Her *Wool Gathering* issues #20 and #21 (now *Spun Out* #8) on hats provided basic construction information for tams and urged knitters to feel free to experiment with the top of the hat, instead of planning it. According to Elizabeth, anything one decides to try will be unique and interesting. A picture of some of Elizabeth's lovely tams can be found in her *Knitting Workshop* (pp. 134–35). These were the first wheel-patterned tams I ever encountered.

My first few constructions were wearable, but were not the beautiful creations I envisioned. I could not seem to get the ideas from my head onto my needles. One evening, while puzzling through this problem, the kaleidoscopes of my childhood came to mind. Suddenly I had

1

the solution to my problem. By graphing only one section of the pattern and duplicating it in the other sections (just as the kaleidoscope does), I could produce and predict the entire design. This gave me a tool for creating symmetrical, unified designs of unlimited scope because I could vary both the patterns and the number of sections used. The close relationship between the shaping of the top of the tam and the color patterns produces the characteristic appearance of these tams, which are called *wheel-patterned* because of the spoke-like design and structure.

I now use kaleidoscopes to inspire my tam designs and to help solve construction problems. My teleidoscope is especially useful. A teleidoscope is a kaleidoscope that has a spherical lens on the end, but lacks the case that contains the brightly colored pieces from which the image develops. Aim a teleidoscope at anything, and it will reflect it in multi-images. In addition to using this lens to see how ordinary things can turn into extraordinary designs, I can put together a collection of yarns and see how they will look in a tam.

A SHORT HISTORY OF TAMS

When we discuss wheel-patterned tams, we must consider both the shape of the tam and its color patterning. Over the centuries, the structure and the decoration evolved separately, but they came together in the Shetland Islands, off the coast of Scotland.

The origins and shaping of knitted tams

Hats, caps, and socks are among the oldest knitted artifacts found in Europe. According to Richard Rutt, author of *A History of Hand Knitting*, cap knitting was well established in England and Scotland by the early 1400s. By that time, knitting in Europe incorporated intricate shaping and elaborate colorwork.

The beret, predecessor to the tam, was a common style of hat in Europe during the Renaissance. Many knitted berets believed to have been made in the mid-sixteenth century have been found in mainland Europe and in England; these hats were knitted very large and then felted. All examples demonstrate their makers' knowledge of technical details, such as shaping, and are of a single color (although some were lined in a second color).

The direction in which these berets were worked varies. Some were made from the top down, with stitches increased to the desired width and then decreased at the brim. Others were made from the brim up, with stitches increased to the desired width and then decreased, by various methods, to the center of the top.

Fair Isle color patterns

The earliest examples of what we call Fair Isle color patterning which have been found in Scotland are two caps and two purses which date from around 1850, although older descriptions of colorful Shetland hosiery exist. One cap and one purse were made of silk; the others were made of wool. These examples are heavily patterned with "OXO" designs (formed with alternating circular and cross-like shapes) and demonstrate a brilliant use of color.

They were not made in Scotland, but probably came from one of the Baltic countries—Norway, Sweden, Finland, Latvia, Estonia, or Lithuania. The materials and dyes used, as well as the complex colorwork and technique, suggest this origin. By 1800 stranded color-pattern knitting was becoming popular around the Baltic Sea and there was a flourishing trade between the Shetland Islanders and their Baltic neighbors. No doubt the techniques of knitting and other crafts were traded along with actual products.

Alice Starmore, author of *Alice Starmore's Book of Fair Isle Knitting*, believes that all of the OXO color patterns considered typical of the Shetland Islands originated with the hats imported from the Baltic countries. Similar hats seen in Shetland Island museums but believed to have been made later in the nineteenth century show much less elaborate colorwork and less refined technique. They were made of materials available on the islands, which suggests that islanders produced them. Starmore speculates that these later hats were copies of the older garments and that the designs evolved as knitters varied the original themes.

Rutt suggests that the OXO patterns developed after samples of craftwork (including knitted pieces) from the Baltic areas were seen in the Shetland Islands and then copied into the islanders' prevailing handcraft, knitting. Both Rutt and Starmore believe that the intricacies now seen in Fair Isle colorwork were devised through experimentation as well as in response to market demand. The first Island-made color pattern work adorned hats, gloves, and stockings.[1]

---

[1]Obviously, a short discussion cannot do justice to the development and beauty of Fair Isle knitting. For a more thorough history, see the books by Alice Starmore and Richard Rutt.

The upper tam, "Fire-fly Fantasy," displays a pattern developed from the "leaves and buds" idea explained on page 41. The design of the lower tam is based on a simple heptagon (page 37).

The upper tam, "Grandma's Garden," shows garland patterning, which is explored beginning on page 70. The lower tam, "Plum Pizzicato," demonstrates patterning of the "floral" or "petal" type (page 40).

Wheel-patterned tams

No doubt the first color-patterned tams seen in Scotland resulted from a marriage between the color designs in the Baltic silk hat and the typical Scots bonnet, a felted beret.

Tams became popular with young English ladies during the late Victorian period. Fair Isle wheel-patterned tams were first introduced in the 1930s, and have retained their popularity longer than other types of tams.

THE IDEA OF THE TAM
The shape

A tam is a knitted bag shaped in a particular way while it is being worked, then blocked to its final shape after it is complete. In the past tams were most often knitted from the center out, an approach which allows the increases to occur almost invisibly amid the beautiful patterning. Today, in contrast, tams are more commonly knitted from the ribbing to the top, and all sorts of decorative decreasing techniques adorn them.

The construction methods and sizing for tams knitted from ribbing to top can vary widely. One type of tam increases gently until it reaches its full width, then decreases gently to its center. Another type increases to its full complement of stitches right after the ribbing, includes about 4 inches of straight knitting, and then regularly decreases to the center. I think of this as the "basic" tam because it is the shaping method most frequently used today. Some tams are worked with all the increases and decreases occurring in the straight rows between the color patterns; this is a technique often used to shape sweaters with patterned yokes.

In its simplest form, a tam knitted from ribbing to center in what I consider the "basic" way begins with enough stitches to go around the head. These are worked for 1 inch in ribbing. Then a large number of increases in a single row brings the tam to its maximum number of stitches. These stitches are worked evenly until the tam measures 3 to 4 (or even more) inches from its beginning. The tam is finished by working decreases until the center top is reached. The decreases on the top can be worked in several ways, which will be explained in Part 2, Tam Basics, and in Part 6, Variations.

A tam achieves its characteristic shape when the completed tam is washed, and then allowed to dry while stretched on a dinner plate, heavy cardboard form, or tam stretcher.

Color patterns

The straight knit area above the ribbing, or body, can contain several inches of color-patterned bands, also called *border* patterns. And the knitter may also decorate the top of the tam (the decreasing area) with color patterns, also known as *wheel* patterns. I use traditional Fair Isle borders; the design of the wheel patterns is the part of tam knitting that particularly interests me.

MATERIALS
Yarn

Yarn selection is important to the success of any knitting project. Buy the best yarn that you can afford. My tams have been designed using the beautiful and authentic Shetland wool from Scotland. This wool is the best weight for my purposes and comes in a broad selection of colors. I prefer what is called "Shetland jumper weight" because its fine gauge and extensive palette permit subtle and marvelously colored patterns. For me, it works up at a gauge of 7 stitches per inch on size 3 (3.25 mm) needles, and at a gauge of 8 stitches per inch on size 2 (2.75–3 mm) needles. Shetland jumper weight yarn runs 150 yards/ounce, which makes it the equivalent of a *Class A*, or fingering weight, yarn. You may substitute a different yarn of similar weight.

Class B and *Class C* yarns, sport and worsted weights, can be used if you consider how the yarn thickness will affect the drape of the tam and the sizes of the color patterns. For example, a tam made of a Class C or worsted weight yarn (5 stitches=1 inch, 49 yards/ounce), will appear very different from a tam made to the same dimensions out of Shetland yarn. In the heavier yarn, the thickness of the stranded knitting will not allow the tam to fall cleanly into the characteristic disk shape and the tam will appear smaller than its knitted dimensions would suggest. In order to fit like the tam made from fingering yarn, the tam in worsted weight yarn will need to be larger from the ribbing to the top.

Wool has the elasticity needed to block the wheel patterns effectively. Acrylic and acrylic combinations do not block well. Avoid disaster; *do not mix types of yarn in one tam*. A combination of yarns of different composition will not block properly. I have learned, from bitter experience, not to include even a small bit of a different yarn just because I want to use a few leftover yards of rose.

Experimentation with any fiber other than wool must carefully consider the characteristics of that fiber. For example, I have used alpaca yarns in both sport and worsted weight. Color patterns are especially lovely worked in the sport weight. But alpaca does not have the elasticity of wool and will not hold the beret shape well. The tam will drape, rather than sit, on the head. Although this effect differs from that of a tam made from Shetland yarn, it is still attractive. The ribbing of an alpaca tam needs elastic cord to maintain its shape.

The number of colors you will need depends on how complicated you want your tam to be. Solid-color tams are attractive; two colors are enough to allow for patterning. But I find that more colors are more satisfying. I generally pick three basic background colors and two or three pattern colors. Then I select a final color as a contrasting highlight. There's more about color in Part 5.

A tam made of Shetland wool requires about 2 ounces of yarn. You will need at most 1 ounce of the main color, plus smaller amounts of the other colors. Shetland yarn is generally sold in 1-ounce skeins of about 150 yards, so buy one skein of each color you need. If your yarn shop stocks cones, you may be able to have ¼ or ½ ounce (38 yards or 75 yards) measured off if you need very small quantities of certain colors. You will want ½ ounce of each supplementary color and ¼ ounce of the contrast color.

In a Class B or sport weight yarn, you will need about 3 ounces in all. Figure on about 1½ ounce for the main color and slightly less for each additional color.

When using Class C or worsted weight yarns, you will need a total of about 4 ounces. Figure on about 2 ounces for the background color that you will also use for the ribbing, and less for the other colors. You will need a few yards of the contrast color.

Save every scrap of wool, because the color patterns sometimes require only a small amount of a special color to set off the design. Occasionally I use small pieces to add highlights in the wheel pattern through duplicate stitching or Swiss embroidery (see the Techniques section). Because I don't enjoy duplicate stitching, I plan to knit most of these highlights into my designs.

Tams knitted in different weights of yarns: the untitled star tam, at the upper right, was worked in Shetland yarn and "Brown's Woods," on the bottom, in worsted weight. The heather green tam shows the decreasing technique I use most often: double decreases worked at seven points around the top on every other row.

Equipment

You will need a *16-inch circular needle* of the size which gives you the appropriate gauge. I usually use a size 3 (3.25 mm) for tams made of Shetland yarn (fingering weight). Class B (sport weight) usually requires a size 5 (3.75–4 mm) needle and Class C (worsted weight), a size 7 (4.5–5 mm) needle. Double-pointed needles of the same size will be needed to close the tam, because the decreases make it difficult at a certain point to continue using the circular needle. The ribbing will take a circular needle two sizes smaller than the one for the main body of the tam. If you plan to use a tubular cast on, you will need a third circular needle, one or two sizes smaller than the needle used for the ribbing (size 0 circular needles are reasonably common; if you need a smaller size, a few mail-order sources have 16-inch circular needles to size 0000, or you may have to use a set of double-pointed lace needles).

Knitters' graph paper (see the Source List) will make your design tasks easier. If you have tried graphing your designs on regular graph paper, you have found that the design when knitted looks horizontally compressed. That is because knitted stitches are rectangular, not square. Knitters' graph paper is ruled in rectangles, not squares, so you can draw your designs and know *exactly* how they will look when knitted. All graphs in this book use knitters' graph paper.

Elastic cord can be inserted into the bottom of a tam's ribbing to help hold its shape. Although I have never needed it on a Shetland wool tam, I have used it with alpaca and other less elastic fibers. I use a tubular rib cast on, making extra slip-stitch rows for a casing. During the finishing process I attach a safety pin to the end of the elastic cord and pull it through the casing at the bottom of the ribbing. I adjust the elastic to fit, knot it securely, remove the pin, trim the excess elastic, and ease the knot gently back into the casing.

For *stitch markers*, I usually use knitters' pins or loops of yarn in a contrasting color. Also handy are scissors, safety pins, and large-eyed sewing needles, both blunt and sharp.

A *tam stretcher* of the desired size will be needed to block the tam to its characteristic shape. I use a 10-inch dinner plate. The only drawback is that drying a tam on a plate takes a long time, since air doesn't circulate very well around and through it. A tam stretcher has holes to facilitate quicker drying. You can make a tam stretcher from masonite or plywood in the size that you prefer, or just cut a circle from stiff cardboard.

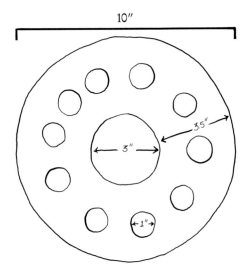

10″

3.5″

3″

1″

You can use a plate to stretch your tams while they dry, or you may want to make a tam stretcher. The dimensions here are suited for a 10-inch tam. The stretcher is made from ¼-inch plywood. The edges are beveled, and the holes allow air to flow through the tam. There are 1-inch holes around the edge and a 3-inch hole in the center.

A *plate rack or stand* is a lovely way to display the beautiful wheel-patterned tams that you design. I display new tams as they dry and sometimes longer. Tams to be shown on the wall may be framed with large quilting hoops or wire frames of the desired dimensions.

TECHNIQUES
Color-pattern knitting

Tams are knitted in the round. The right side of the knitting will be toward you at all times, making it easy to keep track of your color patterns. You will knit every round, producing a stockinette fabric (as opposed to alternately knitting and purling in flat knitting).

Patterns in the Fair Isle tradition limit the use of colors to two per row. You will need to practice knitting with two colors at once. Many people knit with one color in each hand as I do; others knit carrying both colors in one hand, using one or two fingers. For me the first method is much easier. If you have not done color pattern knitting before, I encourage you to practice knitting a swatch of garter stitch carrying your yarn in the hand you don't usually use.[2]

---

[2]There are a number of resources with good instructions for carrying two colors and weaving in. Two possibilities are Jacqueline Fee's *The Sweater Workshop* (Loveland, Colorado: Interweave Press, 1983), pp. 31–37, and *Alice Starmore's Book of Fair Isle Knitting* (Newtown, Connecticut: Taunton Press, 1988), pp. 94–96.

There are two basic rules you should keep in mind, especially if you are just beginning to do Fair Isle knitting. Knit rounds with *no more than two colors* at once. Also, carry your yarn *no farther than 1 inch.* Longer carries are difficult to tension properly and will slow you down.

You will not "pick up each color under the color before" as is normally requested in color-pattern knitting. The color not in use may float *loosely* behind the other without being woven in. The key word here is loosely; yarn carried too loosely may be fixed later, but yarn carried too tightly cannot.

Weaving in

Weaving in is a technique that catches and secures the strand of a long carry. You will not need to use it unless you carry the yarn across more than 1 inch of stitches. In the fingering weight yarn, 1 inch is about 7 stitches; in sport weight, it is 6 stitches; and in worsted weight, 5 stitches. The technique differs according to which hand carries the yarn to be woven in. I try to plan my designs to avoid weaving in.

Duplicate stitching

Sometimes when a tam is completed, you will note small mistakes in the color pattern or you will want to add a little color. Duplicate stitching, or Swiss embroidery, may be used sparingly to add highlights or to correct mistakes. This type of stitching is best done after the tam has been placed on a stretcher; stitching is easier, because the tam is under tension and the stretcher is between your needle and the tam's lower surface.

Reading graphs

Each stitch is represented by a rectangle, and each round of knitting is represented by a row of rectangles. I have graphed only a two-color pattern here, because you will work with two colors in each row. When you make a tam, of course, you may use a variety of colors—but if you stick to the Fair Isle concept, you will use only two at a time. As you knit, you can change the background and foreground colors at planned intervals.

For border patterns in the straight-knit body of the tam, you read the graphs from right to left and from bottom to top starting at the right-hand ↑ (see graph 1). The left-hand ↑ marks the point where the pattern

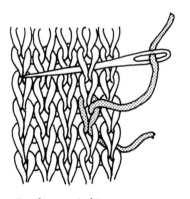

Duplicate stitching

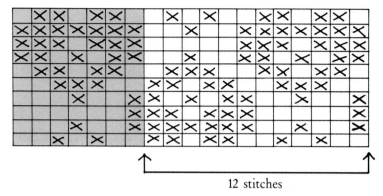

12 stitches

1
This is the way graphs are written for border patterns. Start read-
ing at the righthand arrow. Read from right to left, bottom to
top. Knit the area which is not shaded; the shaded stitches show
how the repeats connect with each other.

repeats. A partial repeat is shown in the shaded area, so you can see how
the pattern connects with itself.

Special considerations apply to reading the wheel pattern graphs (see
graph 2). If you start at the right bottom corner and read across in the
conventional way, making your decreases at the ends of the rows, the
jog in the pattern that occurs where rounds join will be emphasized by
the decrease ridge. To avoid this, and to effectively hide the jog, here's
how to read the graphs for the wheel segments.

The beginning of the round starts at the center of the pie-shaped
section (see ↑). Read each pattern round starting at the ↑. Read to the
left until you reach the end of the section. Then go to the far right of
the graph and knit the single stitch in the column at the right-hand edge.
Return to the pie-shaped section and read to the left again until you reach
the last rectangle before the ↑.

For the second round move up to the next line of rectangles, starting at the ↑ position. When the graph narrows by a stitch at both ends,
make a double decrease. The single stitch at the side of the graph appears as the center point of the double decrease on decrease rounds. In
the pattern for the basic tam, you will make double decreases at seven
points on the third, fifth, seventh, ninth, and so on, rounds. Notice the
staircase effect on the graph.

2
This is the way graphs are written for wheel patterns to be worked in the decrease area. This graph is set up to be used with double decreases worked every two rounds. There are 26 stitches at the base of each segment, and 26 rounds in the wedge. Stitches to be worked are in the unshaded area; the particular stitches referred to in each caption are light gray. The shape of the wheel segment is indicated by medium-gray shading. As the decreases are worked, the wheel segment gets narrower.

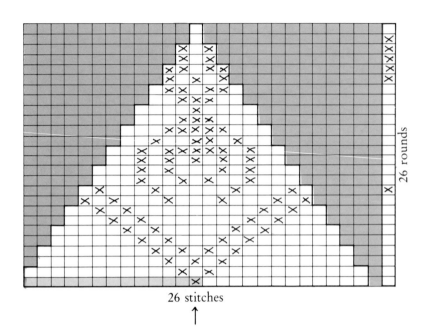

26 rounds

26 stitches

↑

Start reading at the arrow in the center of the first round, and read to the left, working the stitches shown by the light gray tint.

Continue the first round at the far right by working the single stitch, then return to the wedge shape and complete the first round, stopping on the stitch before the center arrow.

↑

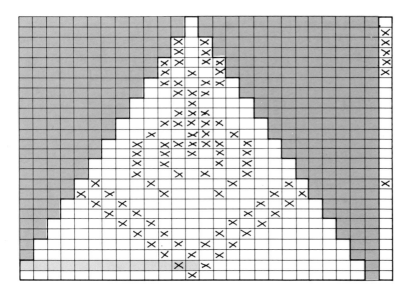

Begin the second round by moving up a row and beginning with the stitch over the center arrow. Continue reading the graph as you did for the first round.

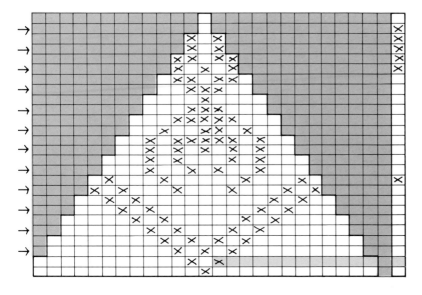

double decrease on rounds marked with arrows

On rows where stairsteps are indicated, work double decreases. The single stitch at the far righthand side of the graph will appear as the center of the double decrease.

Tubular cast on for k1, p1 rib

The tubular cast on produces a neat, rounded, elastic edge without the corded edge of the usual methods.[3] The more I use this cast on the more I like it. It is especially useful when working with alpaca or other fibers that do not have the elasticity of wool; by knitting 4 or 6 rows in Step 4, I can produce a casing at the bottom of the ribbing which allows me to insert elastic cord to help the ribbing hold its shape.

1. Cast on in *scrap yarn* of a contrasting color *half* of the required stitches plus 1 stitch. You will need an odd number of stitches.
2. Using a needle one or two sizes smaller than the tam needle and the *tam yarn*, knit one row.[4]
3. *Knit 1, purl into the running thread between the stitches*; repeat from * to * until you reach the last stitch, then purl into the running thread and the last stitch together. Join into a circle, being careful not to twist.
4. *Round 1:* *Knit 1, yarn forward, slip 1 purlwise, yarn back*. Repeat * to *. *Round 2:* *Yarn back, slip 1 purlwise, yarn forward, purl 1*. Repeat * to *. Alternate rounds 1 and 2 for 4 to 6 rounds.
5. Change to your tam needle and k1, p1 for 1 inch.
6. When the tam is complete, carefully cut out the scrap yarn used for the first row.

---

[3]For other ways of obtaining the same tubular effect see the article by Montse Stanley listed in the bibliography.
[4]If you use a long-tail cast on, you can do steps 1 and 2 at the same time. Tie the scrap yarn and the tam yarn together with a slip knot. Then cast on, with the scrap yarn going over your thumb, and the tam yarn going to the back. Don't count the slip knot as one of the cast-on stitches.

ABBREVIATIONS

dbl dec – double decrease. This procedure makes three stitches into one, eliminating two stitches. In this book I use the following method: slip two stitches knitwise together, knit 1, pass the two slipped stitches over. In this case the center stitch, which is also the second slipped stitch, will remain on the top, forming a slightly raised vertical line.[5]

DBL DEC

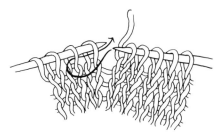

1
Slip two stitches knitwise together.

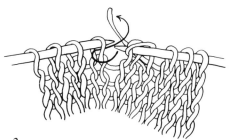

2
Knit one.

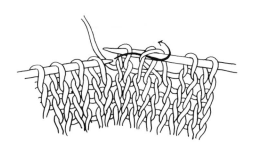

3
Pass the two slipped stitches over.

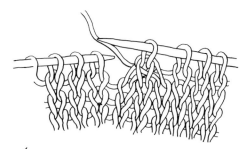

4
Completed decrease.

---

[5]The first slipped stitch is the blank at the left of the graph, where the stairstep occurs; the second slipped stitch is the separate stitch at the right of the graph. The knit stitch is the blank at the right of the graph, also a stairstep.

K2TOG

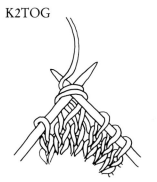

Knit two stitches together.

k—Knit.

k2tog—Knit 2 stitches together. This is the mirror image of *ssk* and leans to the right.

inc—Raised bar increase. Insert the left needle from front to back under the bar (horizontal or running thread) between the stitches and knit through the back of it. One stitch is increased (see sketch).

p—Purl.

psso—Pass slipped stitch over.

p2sso—Pass two slipped stitches over.

ssk—Slip 2 stitches knitwise separately to right needle, insert left needle from the left side into the front of the slipped stitches and then knit them together. This is a mirror image of *k2tog* and leans to the left.

INC (RAISED BAR INCREASE)

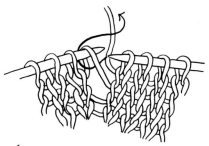

1
Insert left needle from front to back under the bar between the stitches.

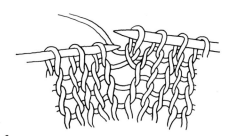

2
Knit through the back of the picked-up bar.

SSK

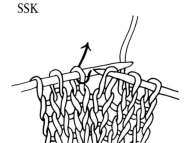

1
Slip two stitches knitwise separately to the right needle.

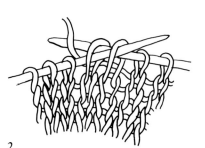

2
Insert left needle from the left side into the fronts of the slipped stitches.

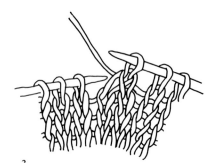

3
Knit them together.

PART 2
Tam Basics

Tams can be made in all sizes, shapes, and patterns, but you don't need to master all the possibilities before you pick up your needles. This section gives basic instructions for making a plain, 10-inch–diameter tam, to fit a head which measures 21 inches around, using Shetland, sport, or worsted weight yarn. The tam described here is the "essential" tam, using my favorite method of decreasing for the top: double decreases on alternate rows, at seven points around the tam. There's also information on washing and blocking your completed tam.

The structure of the tam is given in standard knitting pattern format; a short discussion of adding color patterns follows.

But that's just the beginning. If you want to make a tam for someone whose head is larger or smaller than 21 inches, or if you want a different size of tam, Part 3, Special Sizing for Basic Tams, will give you information on changing the dimensions. If you want to develop proficiency in designing and using color patterns, Part 4, Wheel Patterns for the Basic Tam, describes this aspect of tam-making in detail. Part 5, Color, talks about how to choose colors to use in your patterns. And Part 6, Variations, describes other ways to shape and finish the tops of tams.

THE BASIC 10-INCH TAM

These instructions are written for Shetland yarn (150 yards/ounce); directions for using sport weight (75 yards/ounce) and worsted weight (50 yards/ounce) yarns are included in brackets.

Hat diameter: 10 inches.
Head circumference: 21 inches.
Stitch gauge: 7 sts=1 inch, [6 sts=1 inch], [5 sts=1 inch].
Row gauge: 11 rows=1 inch, [8 rows=1 inch], [6 rows=1 inch].

Yarn: 2 ounces Shetland yarn, [3 ounces sport weight], [4 ounces worsted weight].

Needles: 16-inch circular needle to achieve gauge, try size 3 [size 5], [size 8]; double-pointed needles of the same size; 16-inch circular needle two sizes smaller for the ribbing; and (optional) 16-inch circular needle one or two sizes smaller than the ribbing needle for tubular cast on.

Ribbing

Using smaller needle, cast on 144, [112], [92] stitches. Use any method; if you plan to do a k1, p1 ribbing, you might like to try the tubular cast on (see Techniques). Place a marker to show the end of the round. Join the edges carefully so that they are not twisted.

Work k2, p2 ribbing (if you have used a regular cast on) or k1, p1 ribbing (with either tubular or regular cast on) for 1 inch.

Body

Change to larger needle. Increase evenly in next round until stitches equal 182, [168], [140]. The increase sequence for Shetland yarn is *k3 use inc 1 in next st*, working 2 extra increases at random to bring the total to 182 sts. The increase sequence for sport and worsted yarns is *k1, inc in next st*. In worsted weight, work 2 extra increases at random to achieve a total of 140 sts.

Work even in stockinette stitch until body (straight knit portion) measure 3½, [3½], [3¼] inches. On the last row, divide your work into seven equal segments: *K26, [24], [20], place marker*, repeat around. The decreases will occur in the center of each segment. While this may seem overly complicated–why not simply decrease at the beginning or end of each segment?–the reasoning will become clear when you start adding color patterns on your next tam. Be sure that the segment markers can be easily distinguished from the end-of-round marker.

Decrease for the top, or wheel

The method described here is the one I prefer for a patterned tam, since it produces a straight ridge along the decrease line that doesn't detract from the color patterning. Other methods, which produce more distinctive textured effects, are described in Part 6, Variations. *Decrease at seven points using a double decrease:* You will have seven decrease points, and will use a double decrease (dbl dec) at each of these points on every other

THE ANATOMY OF THE TAM

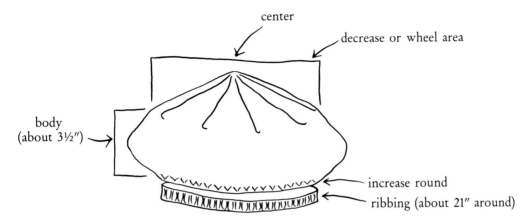

round. The dbl dec is worked as follows: slip 2 knitwise together (the second stitch will always be the marked ridge), K1, p2sso.

Round 1: *K12, [11], [9], dbl dec, k11, [10], [8]*.

Round 2: Knit.

Round 3: *K11, [10], [8], dbl dec, k10, [9], [7]*.

Round 4 and other even-numbered rounds: Knit.

Round 5 and other odd-numbered rounds: Continue to work decrease rounds, as in rounds 1 and 3, but on each succeeding round, knit one less stitch before and after the decrease points than in the previous decrease round. Decrease until 14 stitches remain, then work

Final round: *K1, dbl dec*, end with k2tog.

Complete tam

Break yarn, leaving about 5 inches, and draw through the remaining stitches. Pull yarn through the center to the inside and weave in all ends. Block (see instructions below).

Care and blocking

Caring for tams is simple. Hand wash in lukewarm water in a good liquid soap. Shampoo works well and smells nice, too. If you like, a few drops of cream hair conditioner or Lano Rinse™ in the cold rinse water can soften the fibers. Place the tam between towels and press out some of the moisture. *Please do not wring.*

The decrease area of the basic tam has been shaped with double decreases every two rows. Note the straight lines between segments, and the slightly raised stitch at the center of the decrease. The tam is shown in color on page 9.

Block by gently stretching and smoothing over a dinner plate or tam stretcher about 10 inches in diameter. Place the wheel pattern on the back (convex side) of the plate and the ribbing on the front (concave side). Center the wheel pattern on the plate by gathering up the ribbing on the other side. Set the tam stretcher away from heat and allow the tam to dry *completely* before removing the plate. Turn the plate over frequently, or set it on its side. Drying will take a day or two, depending on the humidity, type of stretcher used, and thickness of yarn.

ADDING COLOR PATTERNS TO THE BASIC TAM

There are two places to think about adding color patterns to the tam, and you can work with either or both: the body (or straight knit area

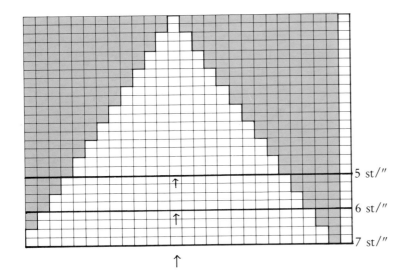

5 st/"

6 st/"

7 st/"

Graph for wheel segment shaped with double decreases worked every two rows. This graph can be used for all three weights of yarn; count rows from the top down.

weight	gauge	stitches at start of segment	use this number of rows
worsted	5 st/"	18	18
sport	6 st/"	22	22
Shetland	7 st/"	26	26

above the ribbing), and the wheel (or decrease area for the top). Once you are familiar with the principles, you can experiment with the patterning, the shaping of the tam, and the number of stitches at each stage in order to develop a unique design. For your first tams, it's simplest to add patterning which doesn't require modifications.

On the basic tam, with the stitch counts described above, you can start by selecting border designs. You can design your own patterns, or select one from group A and one from group B at the back of the book (pages 84–90). Choose patterns with repeats that divide evenly into the number of stitches in the body. You may adjust the number of stitches to fit the pattern repeats, but limit your changes to plus-or-minus 1 inch's worth of stitches, and remember to return to the original number of stitches before beginning the wheel pattern. This is called the "fudge factor"! Be sure, too, that the patterns can be completed in the number of rows available at the gauge for your yarn. Plan on separating the color patterns from each other, the ribbing, and the wheel pattern with a few rows of the base color.

If you would like to put color patterning in the top decrease area, select or design a graph for a wheel pattern. More information on designing is given on pages 36–51. For a tam with seven decrease points, many of the graphs in this book are appropriate.

You can work your patterning in two colors, one for background and one for the design, or you can begin to work with additional colors as you proceed with the tam.

PART 3
Special Sizing
for Basic Tams

You don't need to do or understand mathematical formulas in order to be an expert tam maker. The concepts involved in tam design can be understood through visual means *or* by using a calculator.

The only essential measurement for fitting a tam is the head size; other measurements are a matter of personal taste and style. This section will give you control so that *your* personal taste and style can affect the shape of your tams.

Math sometimes does help, and I will give formulas which you may find useful, although I am basically a person who envisions results and then makes them happen. I have struggled over the years to use mathematical concepts in my tam making, and to some degree I have failed—primarily because knitting is elastic and tams don't need to fit exactly. Most mathematical absolutes, therefore, are not necessary. I also prefer to "think knitting" rather than work formulas; however, knowing how to do the math is convenient at times.

The special sizing suggestions that follow have been checked using various head sizes and dimensions. It is assumed that the wheel pattern is formed by using the double decrease every other row.

CHANGING THE HEAD SIZE

People's heads are different sizes...but not much different, so head sizing is easy to change. The basic pattern is written for a head circumference of about 21 inches. Head circumference determines the number of stitches in the ribbing of the tam; fortunately, if you need to make a tam for someone who has a larger or smaller head, enlarging or reducing the size of the ribbing is simple.

Measure the head, and multiply its circumference in inches by the stitch gauge of the yarn you are using. Cast on 80% of that number and work the ribbing. (Ribbing calls for 80% of the stitches in the full measurement, since ribbing stretches and you want a reasonably snug fit.)

head size (around the ears) = _____
head size × stitches/inch = number of stitches in full circumference
number of stitches × .80 = stitches to cast on for ribbing

After working the ribbing, increase to the number of stitches required for the body in the yarn you are using. This may be one of the numbers in the basic tam or a number you have determined through the modifications outlined in later parts of this book.

CHANGING THE FINISHED DIAMETER OF THE TAM: GETTING READY

The other major dimension which you may want to alter is the finished diameter of the tam. This isn't a one-step change, like the head circumference, but you can alter the diameter through a logical and easy process, once you understand it.

First, you need to decide how large you want your tam to be. Finished diameters of average tams range from 9 inches (quite small) to 12 inches (generous). Even a ½-inch change will be noticeable.

You can use a tape measure or samples of muslin to try different sizes on your head. This will be an approximate process, but will give you an idea of what you want. Larger tams are more floppy and dramatic, and can be pulled down farther over the ears. Keep in mind that you will also need to have a plate or make a stretcher of the appropriate diameter on which to block your finished tam.

desired diameter of tam = _____ inches

The holistic tam

When you want to change the finished diameter, you encounter the holistic tam. All the parts of the tam other than the ribbing interact very closely to determine the finished size. Talking about this is a challenge; it even requires that we define and name the parts of this unique style

THE PARTS OF THE TAM
AND HOW THEY WORK TOGETHER

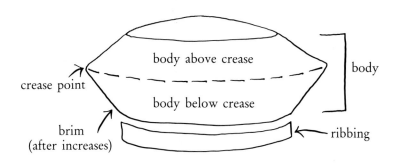

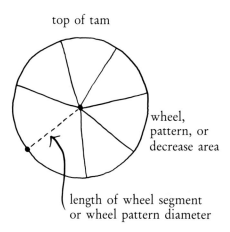

of hat before we begin our discussion. The process is complicated because each area flows smoothly into the next, and because measurements and benchmarks before blocking are very different from those after blocking. There is a worksheet on pages 78–80 which will be useful for keeping track of the decisions you make when designing your own tams. Photocopy it, and use it both for planning your tams and for keeping records of your results.

We begin, therefore, with the anatomy of the tam. There are four basic parts:

Ribbing: This is a relatively independent element; its size is determined by the head circumference of the tam wearer.

Brim: This refers to the area just above the ribbing, after the full number of increases has been made.

The "brim" is the hardest part of the tam to think about, because it exists primarily as a concept. The ribbing moves almost immediately into the body; the brim is a transitional point which plays an important role in calculations, but because of take-up (during knitting) and blocking (afterward) cannot be measured on the tam in progress, or in the finished tam.

The *amount of increase* after the ribbing (which results in the number of stitches in what we're calling the brim) is a critical factor in determining the finished diameter. We will discuss both *brim circumference* and *brim diameter.*

A TAM BEFORE AND AFTER BLOCKING

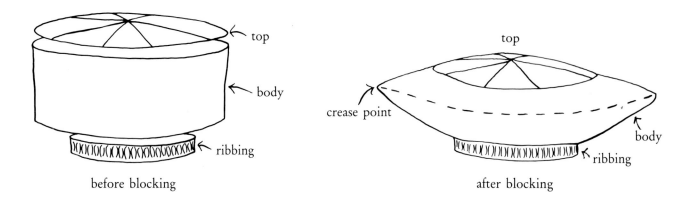

before blocking

after blocking

Body: This is the straight knit area between the increases above the ribbing and the start of the decreases for the top. The *length* of the body is important to the tam's final shape, and is one of the numbers you will need to determine.

When the tam is blocked, the crease which defines the hat's finished diameter appears—almost magically—within the body area. After blocking, the body's length is divided into two sections: the *length below the crease point* (on the ribbing side of the tam) and the *length above the crease point* (on the top of the tam).

Wheel Area or Pattern: This is also the decrease area for the top; the name reflects its potential for carrying color patterns. We will work with the *wheel pattern diameter*, the *rate of decrease* for the wheel pattern, and the *length of the wheel segment*, which is a function of the rate of decrease.

Materials and gauge

Before making alterations which affect so many aspects of the tam at once, you need to be very familiar with the stitch and row gauge of the yarn you intend to use. If you work in the same yarn most of the time, of course, the work you do now will be a foundation for your future designing.

After choosing the yarn for your tam, make a swatch to determine your stitch and row gauge. Don't assume that yarns of the same class will knit to exactly the same row gauge. Check the specific yarn you will use. For example, Class C yarn (worsted weight) is usually knit to 5 stitches per inch and 7 rows per inch. For me, Brown Sheep Company's "Top of the Lamb," which falls into this class, knits to 5 stitches per inch, but barely 6 rows per inch.

Bear in mind that the tension will be different if you do your gauge on a flat swatch and then knit your tam in the round, and the gauge for color-pattern knitting will be different from the gauge in plain knitting. The ideal swatch, therefore, is knitted in the round using the color pattern you've chosen. If you decide to make an ideal swatch, use a small circular needle and as many stitches as are required to go around it. Measure both the row gauge and the stitch gauge on the *unblocked* sample. Blocking will distort the gauge, particularly on tams.

The row gauge is very important. It will assist you in determining the number of rounds in the body and in the wheel pattern. This is critical when you want to plan color patterns.

stitch gauge = _____ stitches per inch on #_____ needles
row gauge = _____ rows per inch

Increasing above the ribbing, or determining the brim circumference

Now we begin to make major changes. The finished diameter of a tam is determined by the amount of increase after the ribbing, the length of the body of the tam (straight knit portion), and the length of the wheel segment (distance from the beginning of the decreases to the tam's top). These three dimensions interact very closely and can be adjusted to produce your own desired finished diameter.

The *amount of increase* which occurs after the ribbing is the first of these factors, and you'll have to simply decide how much increase you want. There are guidelines, but no firm rules. Most tams are increased a great deal above the ribbing—from 20% up to 100% (for a very floppy tam). I have used increases of 20% to 50%. You can adjust the other parts of the tam to accommodate any amount of increase. (I have not experimented with increases beyond 50%, but they are possible. If you plan to make increases of this type, you will need to increase over several rounds.)

Your choice is not completely arbitrary, because the total number of stitches after the increase affects both the body and wheel sections of the tam. (1) This is the same number of stitches on which you will work the body, and so it determines the maximum circumference of the blocked tam—in other words, how wide the tam can be stretched without distorting the shape of the stitches. (2) In addition, this number of stitches determines the size of the decrease area or wheel section;[6] if you have a lot of stitches to decrease out to reach the center point, you will need a larger area over which to eliminate them.

> 20% increase: *k5, inc*
> 25% increase: *k4, inc*
> 33% increase: *k3, inc*
> 50% increase: *k2, inc*
> For larger increases, use the patterns listed above but repeat them in a second round. The 33% increase will give a 66% increase, and so forth.

> number of stitches in ribbing = _____
> amount of increase = _____%
> number of stitches after increase = _____

To convert the number of stitches after the increase to a measurement in inches, which we will call the *brim circumference*, divide it by your stitch gauge.

$$\frac{\text{number of stitches after increase}}{\text{stitches/inch}} = \text{brim circumference}$$

This number will show up again in a moment and be called C.

> brim circumference (C) = _____ inches

CHANGING THE FINISHED DIAMETER OF THE TAM: MAKING THE ADJUSTMENTS

You now have four numbers. Two have been determined by direct measurement of your swatch:

> stitch gauge
> row gauge

---

[6]When it comes time to plan a wheel pattern, you will find it easier if the number of stitches after the increase is evenly divisible by the number of decrease points that you will use. In the case of the basic tam, with seven decrease points, I increase to 182. In order to accommodate the stitch repeat of a particular border pattern, you can add or subtract a small number of stitches, adjusting the number before you divide the tam into segments and begin to decrease.

THE RELATIONSHIP BETWEEN THE AMOUNT OF
INCREASE AND THE LENGTH OF THE BODY

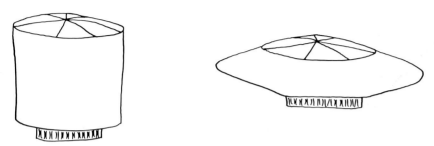

With a small amount of increase, you'll need a long body to produce a well-proportioned tam.

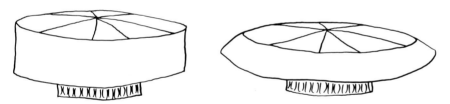

With a large amount of increase, your tam will need a short body.

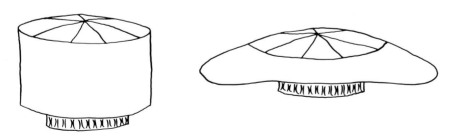

If you increase a fair amount and also knit a long body, you will make a floppy tam.

The other two have resulted from choices you have made:

finished diameter of tam (D)
brim circumference (C)

With these four figures, you can discover how to get all the other parts of the tam to cooperate.

Determining the wheel pattern diameter (W)

You need to figure out how big a circle your wheel pattern, or decrease area, will make. For the basic tam, the graph of the wheel pattern shows the number of rows required to complete the decreases and the pattern.[7] Count the number of rows on the graph, and divide by your row gauge. This will give you the radius of the decrease area and wheel pattern. Multiply the radius by 2 to get the diameter of that pattern in inches.

$$W = 2 \times \frac{\text{number of rows}}{\text{row gauge}}$$

diameter of wheel pattern (W) = _____

Determining the brim diameter (B)

The brim diameter can't be even approximately measured on a tam in progress or a blocked tam. It does have an important effect on the other dimensions of the tam. Take the brim circumference (C), which you have already determined, and divide that number by 3.14 to get the brim diameter in inches. (The number 3.14 is an approximation of *pi*, or π, which represents the geometric relationship between the circumference and diameter of a circle.)

$$B = \frac{C}{3.14}$$

brim diameter (B) = _____ inches

Determining the body length (L)

The magic number you are looking for, the one which makes everything come together, is the body length. This tells you how many inches to

---

[7] If you make more extensive changes in the shape of a tam, you will not be able to count rows on a graph to determine the wheel pattern diameter. The technique to use when you don't have a graph is explained in Part 6.

knit straight between the ribbing and the start of the decreases. You need all the previous figures in order to get this one.

Substitute the values you have determined in the following formula to get the body length in inches:

$$L = D - \frac{B + W}{2}$$

body length (L) = _____ inches

The sketches on the next page show how body length changes in relation to the desired finished diameter. For the purposes of the illustrations, the wheel pattern diameter (W) and brim diameter (B) are the same in each example.

Determining the body length for a different diameter

Once you've gone through this process for one diameter, you can change diameters easily and get new numbers. For example, assume that you have a wheel pattern you like and a head size you like, but you want to play with the idea of a larger or smaller tam.

You start with the basic set of numbers:

D (hat diameter)   = 10.5 inches.
B (brim diameter)   = 8.3 inches.
W (wheel diameter) = 4.7 inches.
        Then L = 4 inches.

If the new diameter is larger than the old, compute the difference between the two diameters and add this difference to the body length. For example, if you want a larger hat, try:

D (new hat diameter) = 11 inches.
New hat diameter is .5 inch larger than basic diameter.
New body length (L) = old body length plus .5 inch.
        Now L = 4 + .5 = 4.5 inches.

If the new diameter is smaller than the old, compute the difference between the two diameters and subtract this difference from the body length. For example, for a smaller hat, try:

D (new hat diameter) = 10 inches.
New hat diameter is .5 inch smaller than basic diameter.
New body length (L) = old body length minus .5 inch.
        Now L = 4 − .5 = 3.5 inches.

How you can change the finished diameter of a tam while keeping the wheel diameter and brim diameter the same: the body length changes.

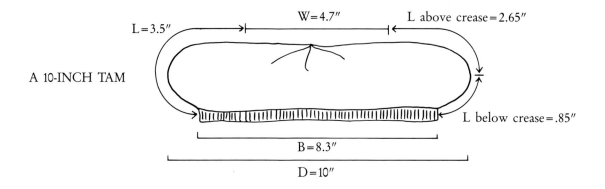

L=3.5″   W=4.7″   L above crease=2.65″

A 10-INCH TAM

L below crease=.85″

B=8.3″

D=10″

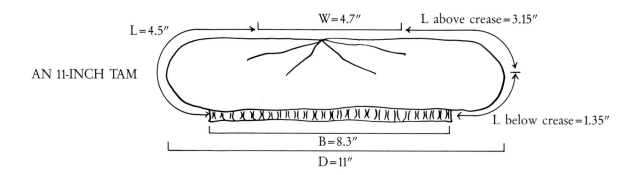

L=4.5″   W=4.7″   L above crease=3.15″

AN 11-INCH TAM

L below crease=1.35″

B=8.3″

D=11″

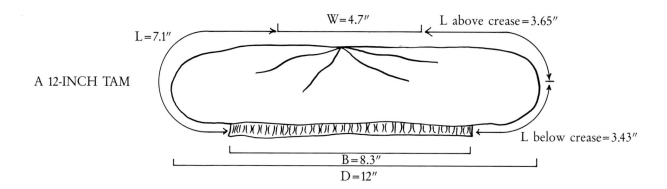

L=7.1″   W=4.7″   L above crease=3.65″

A 12-INCH TAM

L below crease=3.43″

B=8.3″

D=12″

PART 4
Wheel Patterns for
the Basic Tam

Each of us has a unique background of culture, education, and creativity which allows us to make our own contributions to knitting. I receive great pleasure from the design process and encourage you to study my ideas and then develop your own. I'm sure you will find satisfaction both in the process and in the result.

Each tam has a personality of its own. It will take over the design once you begin the wheel pattern. Don't be afraid to do what feels right instead of what is on your graph. Very often, to make a hat fit my sense of artistic rightness, I find it necessary to adapt or scrap old designs or to create new ones. There's a lot of freedom in color knitting, if you'll allow yourself to experience it. As Elizabeth Zimmermann says, "Hold one color in each hand, and it feels rather like painting with two brushes and never having to rinse off either."

I generally limit my own wheel patterns to seven-point patterns. I find the symmetry of the seven-point decrease to be pleasing and unusual. A seven-point decrease produces a shape which we see as very nearly circular. When there is an even number of decrease points, such as six or eight, the eye lines up the elements and sees a hexagon or an octagon, rather than a circular form.

This section will concentrate on designing wheel patterns for the basic tam with seven decrease points. Part 6, Variations, includes information on designing and planning wheel patterns for tams with larger or smaller numbers of decreases, as well as for working garland patterns and incorporating the decreases between the pattern rounds.

The wheel pattern graphs that follow are designed for Shetland yarn.

I find the subtle interplay of color and pattern most pleasant with this weight of yarn. Obviously, you can make wheel patterns using other yarns and I have included several wheel patterns for worsted weight yarns, as well as blank wedges for planning patterns for both worsted and sport weight yarns. Before you knit, remember to check the gauge for which individual wheel graphs have been designed.

USING THE BASIC PATTERN GRAPH

For the pattern with seven decrease points and Shetland weight wool, divide the hat into seven sections of 26 stitches each (a total of 182 stitches). One stitch in each section will appear as the center point for the double decrease—the slightly raised ridge—and the remaining 25 will form the pie-shaped section of the pattern. (Before continuing, please review the note on reading graphs on page 12 in Part 1.)

DESIGNING SHAPES

Repeating a single wedge-shaped motif in each of the segments of the decrease area creates a design with radial symmetry that resembles a kaleidoscope pattern. Several types of seven-sided motifs are possible because of the way a double decrease shapes the knitting, and I use one or more of these as the framework for the patterning of each hat. For the samples here, I've included the pie-shaped graphs for five seven-sided motifs and a sketch of how each pattern will appear on a hat. Study the relationship between the lines on each graph and the lines on its accompanying sketch.

When you are beginning to design a wheel pattern, you will need to be aware of an oddity which affects the relationship between your graphed design and the knitted fabric. If you follow the knitted round on a wheel pattern you find that the decrease point on the fabric not only appears as a ridge raised slightly above the surface; the pattern also jogs slightly toward the center of the tam. The pattern centered on the decrease point forms an angle, and the size of this angle depends on the number of decrease points used to shape the top of the tam. (There's a discussion later on working with more or fewer than seven decrease points.)

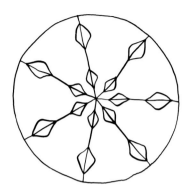

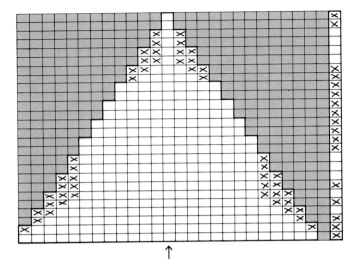

LEAF OR BUD SHAPES

A leaf or bud effect can be produced by placing the points of a star at the decrease line, instead of at the center point (↑) of the wheel segment.

Leaf or bud shapes provide the foundation for the wheel pattern in this tam, "Firefly Fantasy," as well as for "Woodland Fantasy" (see these tams in color on pages 4 and 9).

In designing "Sweet Melodies," shown at the top of the opposite page, I began with the idea of the star shape. I took one element of it, and placed other motifs around it. To get the pattern to work, I placed one extra round at the bottom of the graph.

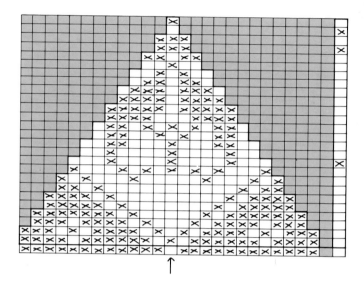

MORE ELABORATE PATTERNS

The shapes described above are only the beginnings of the patterns I work into the tops of my tams. The characteristic kaleidoscopic appearance comes both from the framework (seven-sided decrease structure and the basic shape) and from what I call "inner motifs," or the additional designs I work on the other stitches in each wedge-shaped section.

In one of my favorite tams, called "Sweet Melodies," I began with the idea of the star shape. By comparing the "Sweet Melodies" graph with the basic star, you can see how I used the framework and then created a more complex pattern.

There are many other possibilities for patterning the tops of tams, working with different numbers of decrease points and arrangements of decrease intervals. These changes affect both the structure of the hat and the dynamics of color pattern design, and Part 6, Variations, gives guidelines for further exploration.

Tams in blues, top to bottom: "Sweet Melodies,"
"Jazzy Blues," and an untitled tam.

PART 5
Color

USING COLOR

Entire books have been written about how colors work with each other. I am not an expert in color theory; I have learned about color through knitting. I suspect this is true of many color-pattern knitters. I do know that you must use color to know how it works. Experiment, collect colors, talk to people, take a class in color theory, but most of all, knit with color.

Color is very personal. I tend to work at the blue-rose end of the spectrum and find it difficult to work with the yellow-green end. If you are making a hat for someone, *do not* rely on their descriptions of colors, because these are also personal. It helps to understand whether someone's color preferences have blue or yellow undertones. Most colors, even many naturals, can be described this way. *Always* ask for swatches or to see the clothes with which the tam is to be worn. I carry around a necklace of Shetland yarn butterflies (small skeins) containing all the colors I have on hand. Each sample is labeled with a source and color number. I can then match colors and play with color combinations.

Artists are good sources of information about color combinations. They are usually well schooled (or experienced) in color theory and can predict how a color will change when placed next to another one. For example, I planned one tam in shades of blue, from navy to light blue, with pattern colors changing from natural to white. I planned to use a contrasting bit of strawberry. An artist friend said the color would "die" when used that way and suggested that I use coral. I thought that coral would be too orange but decided to try it anyway. The quantity of blues in the hat grayed the orange of the coral, and the color was successful.

Colored pictures in magazines and books are a good source of inspiration. One of my recent color choices of light rust, gray, black, and natural came from a photograph of birch woods on a very gray day in late fall. A fabric store will sometimes give you small snips of attractive fabrics to add to your color file. And don't forget to check museum collections of fabrics, paintings, rugs, tapestries, porcelain, and pottery.

Play with colors. I stack up balls of colors on my coffee table and study them under different lighting conditions. I patiently rearrange them until I am satisfied with the way they look (or my husband demands space for his coffee cup).

Make swatches to preserve color experiments. Cast on 70 to 90 stitches—enough to go around a 12-inch or 16-inch circular needle—and try any combinations that come to mind. (I don't like using double-pointed needles, but if you'd like to sample with fewer stitches you certainly could.) A friend has several of these swatch "scarves" in the basic colors that she uses and practices new color patterns on the appropriately colored scarf. She leaves the stitches on a thread or on the needle until she needs to experiment again. When using this method, attach tags to each band of patterns noting the colors used, so a good combination can be duplicated.

Another friend reports seeing similar swatch scarves when she talked to knitters in the Shetland Islands. They use them as both a color record and a pattern book. They cast on only about 4 inches' worth of stitches, knotting the colors together at the beginning and end of the row. Although the swatch is flat, the work is not turned and the new row is begun at the right hand edge, after knotting the yarns together.

COLOR IN FAIR ISLE PATTERNS

Fair Isle patterns began to appear during the last half of the nineteenth century. The colors used came from the natural dyes available to the islanders—red from madder, gold and green from lichens and mosses, blue from indigo—and from the natural colors of the Shetland Island sheep, ranging from deep dark brown to fawn and natural.

As chemically dyed colors became available they were incorporated into the designs. Color choices were largely controlled by the markets for which the islanders knit. The more subdued color combinations of the past as well as the more exotic choices seen now are responses to that market. As a result of this experience, the island knitters have a very highly developed sense of color and of how one color relates to another.

When I first began working with Fair Isle patterns, I found it very difficult to choose colors. I found it easier to copy the color combinations of other Fair Isle designs. This may work for you, too. By doing this, I learned how the typical Fair Isle colors shift, how the colors react when placed together, and finally, how to develop an almost three-dimensional patterning.[8] Then I became comfortable with making my own combinations.

Our color choices are often limited to what we have on hand. This can be frustrating, especially if you long to have every color of Shetland yarn ever made. However, this limitation can result in some courageous color experiments and satisfying results. The Fair Islanders had to deal with the same problem. When Michael Pearson asked the Garrick sisters how they chose colors, "They explained that it depended simply on what bits of wool they had lying around. . . . Then, using the largest amount of wool they had as the main color, they started without further ado. . . ." You have only to look at their work to realize that it's possible to combine a multitude of colors with pleasing results.[9]

And so, "without further ado. . . ."

MY FAVORITE COLOR COMBINATIONS

To help you follow the color descriptions here, I have labeled one set of colors as the pattern and one set as the background. In actual use, the pattern colors might become the background colors and vice versa. Some of the combinations are used in the tams shown in this book; in those cases, I've given the tams' names along with the lists of colors.

I will use a 13-row color pattern to illustrate how the colors shift from row to row to create the three-dimensional effect of a Fair Isle pattern. When the colors shade to dark, the pattern appears to recede; when they shade to light, it appears to approach you. A contrasting color is introduced to highlight the center. Sometimes this is a single row and sometimes several rows. This is just one way to work Fair Isle patterns; many others are used, so experiment.

For the best results, the same level of contrast between foreground and background colors should be maintained. If the pattern color is too close in value (determined by the amount of reflected light) to the background color, the pattern can be lost. The striped effect common to Fair Isle

[8]See Sheila McGregor's book for typical Fair Isle color combinations.
[9]Pearson, pp. 136–41.

Two tams in naturals: "Black Star Rising" and an untitled tam. "Black Star Rising" is knitted in alpaca.

patterns can be limited if you maintain the contrast between the foreground and background colors. A change from natural white to pure white can affect the entire color scheme, and on the Shetland Islands, natural white generally is used instead of pure white. The same is true for natural Shetland black (really dark brown) versus dyed black.

Background	Pattern	Contrast
1. Blues		
a. navy	white	garnet
medium blue	natural	strawberry,
sky blue	silver	*or* coral
b. navy	white	
medium blue	cream	
sky blue		
2. Naturals		
a. natural black	white	silver
moorit (brown)	natural	
b. silver	white	
moorit (brown)	natural	
natural black		
3. Greens (illustrated by "Woodland Fantasy")		
a. brown heather	light green heather	pumpkin
light brown heather	brown/green heather	
beige	loden	
b. loden	light yellow heather	robin's egg
dragonfly	honey beige	blue
light green heather	cream/green lovat	
4. Reds (illustrated by "Phoenix of Love")		
a. garnet	white	tartan blue
strawberry	cream	
b. burgundy heather	white	sky blue
garnet	cream	*or* tartan blue
strawberry	gray	
5. Lavenders		
plum	gray	lavender pink
lavender heather	cream	*or* tartan blue
lavender	white	

6. Browns

natural black	cream
moorit (brown)	honey beige
burnt orange heather	light yellow heather

7. Multicolor (illustrated by "Grandma's Garden")

| cream | loden |
| white | green lovat, light green heather, burgundy heather, garnet, strawberry, smoky pink, coral, yellow, medium blue, sky blue, lavender, lavender heather |

Sample 13-row progression in blues: "Sweet Melodies"

	Background	Pattern
Ribbing:	medium blue	
Round	1: navy	gray
	2: navy	gray
	3: medium blue	gray
	4: medium blue	natural
	5: sky blue	natural
	6: sky blue or garnet	white
Center	7: garnet	white
	8: sky blue or garnet	white
	9: sky blue	natural
	10: medium blue	natural
	11: medium blue	gray
	12: navy	gray
	13: navy	gray

Tams in reds, top to bottom: "Ruby Rondo," a plain tam showing the zigzag decrease texture (see page 56), and "Phoenix of Love."

Two tams in lavenders, top and bottom: "Amethyst Adagio" and an untitled tam.

PART 6
Variations

In this section, you will find both variations for the basic tam, and ways to alter every part of it . . . so it's not a basic tam any more. I also endeavor to anticipate any problems you may have when you step beyond the basic instructions, and I offer solutions.

The section begins very simply, with different possibilities for shaping the decrease area of the seven-point tam and for finishing the last few stitches.

Next comes an explanation of how to rearrange the sequence of decreases, and then how to add color patterns to the revised tam. Along the way, you'll learn the secrets behind making a perfectly shaped (flat) tam every time.

This is followed by a discussion on how to make a tam with a larger or smaller number of decreases: both how to structure it, and how to plan a wheel pattern for it. I have chosen as my example a tam with nine decrease points (my preference for an odd number surfaces again), but the principles will work with other numbers of decrease points as well.

You'll also discover here the thought process behind both shape and patterning of a tam I designed, called "Grandma's Garden," which borrows its decrease placement in part from the basic tam (for the rate of decrease) and in part from a round-yoke sweater (for the placement of those decreases).

Finally, the patterning of tams may fascinate you as much as it does me, and you may want to carry it farther. I've knitted very large tams, which I call "wall tams," whose reason for being is the pleasure of their design. Since they have particular requirements, I've outlined their underlying principles.

TOP DECREASE VARIATIONS AND
FINISHING OPTIONS FOR THE BASIC TAM

Other types of top decreases

Although the double decrease worked on every other row is my favorite, other types of decreases produce nine decorative effects, especially on solid-color tams, and may inspire you to experiment with color in different ways. The instructions are written to be used with the seven decrease points of the basic tam, although they can be used with other tam structures as well.

The decreases described on pages 54–56 will cause the decrease line to curve gently to the left or to the right or to zigzag back and forth. Because they make the stitches between the decrease lines lean, their use reduces the depth of the center section. As a result, when you use any of these techniques you will need to knit at least one more inch in the body section of the tam before beginning to decrease for the top.

Choices for center finishes

You can simply pull your final tail of yarn through the stitches at the center top, secure the end, and call the tam finished. Or, you can decorate the top of your tam with one of the following:

1. **Button.** When 14 stitches remain, work even for ½ inch. Then K2tog around. Draw yarn through remaining 7 stitches and gather up. Place 1½-inch button or circular piece of plastic inside the tab, securing with a bit of yarn around the base of the button.
2. **Tab.** When 7 stitches remain, knit even until desired length. End off by drawing yarn through stitches and then through the center.
3. **Pompon.**
4. **Loop.** Work like a tab, but make the knitted extension long enough to be doubled back on itself before you sew its end to the center point of the tam.

1. **Clockwise swirl:** Using a k2tog decrease at each decrease point on every row produces a clockwise swirl pattern in the decrease area. K2tog at seven points every round. The decrease is worked at the end of each wheel segment.

Round 1: *K24, [22], [18] stitches, k2tog*.

Round 2: *K23, [21], [17] stitches, k2tog (the second stitch of the k2tog will be the k2tog of the round before)*.

Round 3 and remaining rounds: On each subsequent round, knit one less stitch before the k2tog. Decrease until 14 stitches remain, then *k2tog*. Finish as usual for basic tam.

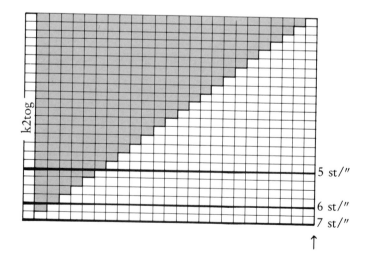

Chart for k2tog decreases; the decreases are worked at the ends of the segments. The chart is marked for use with Shetland, sport, and worsted weight yarns.

2. **Counterclockwise swirl:** Using an ssk decrease at each decrease point on every row produces a counterclockwise swirl pattern in the decrease area. Ssk at seven points every round. The decrease is worked at the beginning of each wheel segment.

Round 1: *Ssk, k24, [22], [18]*.

Round 2: *Ssk (the first stitch of the ssk will be the ssk of the round before), k23, [21], [17]*.

Round 3 and remaining rounds: *Ssk, knit one less stitch after the ssk than in the round before*. Decrease until 14 stitches remain, then *ssk*. Finish as usual for basic tam.

Chart for ssk decreases; the decreases are worked at the beginnings of the segments. The chart is marked for use with Shetland, sport, and worsted weight yarns.

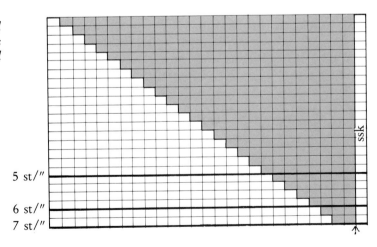

5 st/"

6 st/"

7 st/"

3. **Zigzag:** Alternating the types of decrease—using k2tog for three rounds, then ssk for three rounds—results in a zigzag pattern in the decrease area. Use *k2tog* decrease for 3 rounds and then use *ssk* decrease for 3 rounds. The decreases are worked at the midpoints of each section.

Round 1: *K12, [11], [9] stitches, k2tog, K12, [11], [9]*.

Round 2: *K11, [10], [8] stitches, k2tog (the second stitch of the k2tog will be the k2tog of the round before), k12, [11], [9]*.

Round 3: *K10, [9], [7], k2tog, k12, [11], [9]*.

Round 4: *K10, [9], [7], ssk, k11, [10], [8]*.

Round 5: *K10, [9], [7], ssk (the first stitch of the ssk will be the ssk of the row before), k10, [9], [7]*.

Round 6: *K10, [9], [7], ssk, k9, [8], [6]*.

Round 7: *K9, [8], [6], k2tog, k9, [8], [6]*.

Round 8: *K8, [7], [5], k2tog, k9, [8], [6]*.

Round 9: *K7, [6], [5], k2tog, k9, [8], [6]*. Decrease until 14 stitches remain. Finish with the appropriate ending for the last decrease that you use.

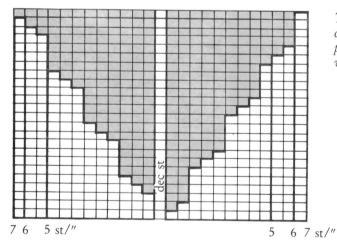

7 6   5 st/″   5   6 7 st/″

This chart shows how the two decreases can be combined; the decreases are worked at the midpoints of the sections. The chart is marked for use with Shetland, sport, and worsted weight yarns.

SHAPING VARIATIONS AND ADDITIONAL SIZING INFORMATION FOR THE BASIC TAM

As you experiment with tam shaping and design, you will need to be able to change dimensions without referring to an existing graph, and to make your own blank graphs and designs. You also may want to explore color patterns with repeats other than those which fit neatly into the basic pattern.

All these freedoms require a more intricate understanding of the relationships between the parts of the tam than you needed in Part 3, Special Sizing for Basic Tams. Again, however, we will be talking about:

brim diameter
length of the body above the crease point
length of the body below the crease point
wheel pattern diameter

We will begin by considering the shaping of the hat, and then cover the small amount of extra information you need in order to plan color patterns.

The relationships between the parts of a tam are best understood if you look at a blocked tam. You will need to look at its top and at its bottom, in separate considerations which you will combine to get the information you need for knitting.

bottom of tam

top of tam

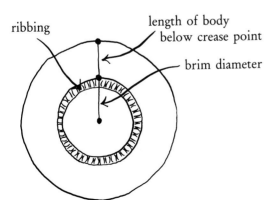

ribbing

length of body
below crease point

brim diameter

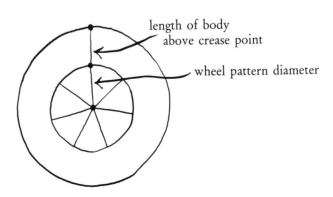

length of body
above crease point

wheel pattern diameter

*The tam on the top is the first one
I made after developing my kaleido-
scopic approach. The lower tam is
"Woodland Fantasy," a recent work.*

The top of the tam is composed of the *wheel pattern diameter* and the *length of the body above the crease point*. The diameter of the wheel pattern varies, depending on the number of stitches at the tam's largest point and the rate of decrease.

For the purposes of figuring changes, the bottom of the tam is composed of the *brim diameter* and the *length of the body below the crease point*.

The basic relationships between these parts can be expressed this way:

$$\frac{\text{finished diameter} - \text{wheel pattern diameter}}{2} = \text{length of body above crease}$$

$$or\ \frac{D - W}{2} = L \text{ above crease}$$

$$\frac{\text{finished diameter} - \text{brim diameter}}{2} = \text{length of body below crease}$$

$$or\ \frac{D - B}{2} = L \text{ below crease}$$

$$\text{length of body above crease} + \text{length of body below crease} = \text{total body length}$$

$$or\ \text{L above crease} + \text{L below crease} = \text{L}$$

Watch the way these parts interact as we make changes in the shaping of the top of the tam.

Altering the arrangement of the decreases: alternative sequence of decreases

You can alter not only the type of decrease, but also the placement of decreases. While I have generally worked decreases on every other row, it is also possible to place the decreases in every third row, every fourth row, or in a combination of different placements.

Let's work through a hat that follows the basic seven-segment pattern, altering the straight-decrease sequence which was used for the wheel pattern in the basic tam. Like the basic tam, this one has a gauge of 7 stitches per inch and 11 rows per inch, a finished diameter of 10 inches, and a maximum of 182 stitches. The basic tam also has the following dimensions, taken from Part 3, Special Sizing for Basic Tams (page 33):

D (hat diameter)   = 10 inches
B (brim diameter)   = 8.3 inches
W (wheel pattern diameter) = 4.7 inches
L (body length)   = 3.5 inches

Plug these numbers into the formulas above, just to see that they work:

$$\frac{D - W}{2} = L \text{ above crease}$$

$$\frac{10 - 4.7}{2} = \frac{5.3}{2} = 2.65$$

$$\frac{D - B}{2} = L \text{ below crease}$$

$$\frac{10 - 8.3}{2} = \frac{1.7}{2} = .85$$

L above crease + L below crease + L
2.65 + .85 = 3.5

When we alter the rate of decrease, we will see changes in W (wheel pattern diameter) and L (body length).

To illustrate, I have arbitrarily chosen to use a double decrease at seven points every *fourth* round until *half* of the stitches have been decreased, then a double decrease at seven points every *second* round until 14 stitches remain.

You can make changes of this type either mathematically or visually. If you prefer simply to work directly with a graph, work out an appropriately shaped wedge on graph paper. This takes more time than the formulas, but for me it is easier. The answer you get from the graphing technique will be one row shorter than the answer from the math technique because when you have knitted the graph to its top line, you will still have a number of stitches left on your needle: there will be one for each segment of the wheel and one for each decrease point. These will be decreased out and finished off in one row, as usual.

The graph here shows my plan for an alternative sequence of decreases; compare it with the "normal" graph on page 23. A straight decrease sequence produces an isosceles triangle at each segment; this new sequence results in curved segments and a slightly less flat tam.

To use the mathematical method of planning this decrease sequence, I first need to determine the *average rate of decrease per row*. Figure this as follows:

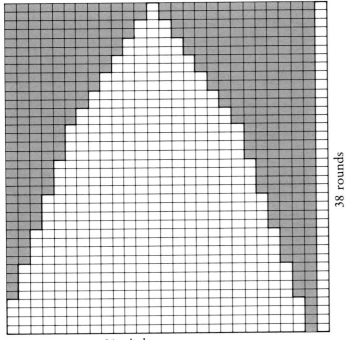

38 rounds

26 stitches per segment

A graph for an alternative sequence of decreases. The chart is one row shorter than the mathematical solution indicates, for reasons which are explained in the text.

$$\frac{\text{number of stitches decreased}}{\text{number of rounds over which decreasing occurs}} = \text{average rate of decrease}$$

In this case, I have two rates of decrease. For the first half of the decreased stitches, I will eliminate 14 stitches every four rounds:

$$\frac{14}{4} = 3.5 \text{ stitches per round}$$

For the second half of the decreased stitches, I will eliminate 14 stitches every two rounds:

$$\frac{14}{2} = 7 \text{ stitches per round}$$

Next, I need to figure out the *wheel pattern diameter*—how big a piece of fabric will be included in the decrease or wheel pattern section of the tam by the time I have worked all my decreases. For the basic tam, we were able to count rounds on a standard graph to get the wheel diameter, but because we have changed the shaping that graph no longer applies.

Let's look at the math involved in knitting this tam. Half of 182 stitches is 91; I will use double decreases every fourth row, at an average of 3.5 stitches per row, until 91 stitches have been eliminated. For the second half of the decreases, I will work double decreases on every second row, at an average of 7 stitches per row, until the remaining 91 stitches have been eliminated.

$$\frac{91}{3.5} = 26 \text{ rows}$$

$$\frac{91}{7} = 13 \text{ rows}$$

I will need 26 + 13 = 39 rows to complete the decreases. This is the radius of the decrease area, or the length of one wheel segment. We need to know the wheel pattern diameter, rather than radius, and we need it in inches, rather than rows. Divide the total number of rows by the row gauge (11/inch) to get the wheel radius in inches, then multiply by 2 to get the wheel pattern diameter:

$$\frac{39}{11} = \text{approx. 3.5 inches} \times 2 = 7 \text{ inches}$$

$$W = 7$$

Now we can use the basic relationships described above to adjust the basic pattern and determine the *length of the body.*

Subtract the diameter of the wheel pattern from the finished tam diameter, and divide by 2 to get the body length above the crease:

$$\frac{D - W}{2} = L \text{ above crease}$$

$$\frac{10 - 7}{2} = \frac{3}{2} = 1.5 \text{ inches}$$

Subtract the brim diameter from the finished tam diameter, and divide by 2 to get the body length above the crease:

$$\frac{D - B}{2} = L \text{ below crease}$$

$$\frac{10 - 8.3}{2} = \frac{1.7}{2} = .85 \text{ inches}$$

Add these two sections to get the total body length:

L above crease + L below crease = L
1.5 + .85 = 2.35 inches

We did it! For a tam with seven decrease points and this new alternative sequence of decreases, the length of the body of this tam will be 2.35 inches, or about 2⅓ inches.

Adding color patterns to the revised tam

There are two places in which to put patterns—the wheel area and the body—and we've changed both of them.

The body is now 2.35 inches long (we'll stick to the decimal version of the number, because math of this type goes most smoothly on a calculator). At 11 rows per inch, we now have the following number of rows for border patterns:

2.35 × 11 = 25.85, or 26 rows

The wheel area is also easy to figure out. You'll want to make yourself a blank graph on which to plan your design. Remember when we computed the number of rows that would be required to complete the decreases for the top? The answer was 39. Make a graph 39 rows tall. Just as in the basic tam, you will begin with 26 stitches in each of the 7 segments, 25 in the wedge and 1 as the decrease point.

Arrange stairsteps to indicate the decreases along the sides of the wedge, in the pattern determined above (every fourth row for the first 26 rows, then every second row for 13 rows). Your graph will look like the one on the next page.

The secrets of the flat tam

Before you begin to rearrange decreases with abandon, you should know that there are guidelines which will give you design freedom and still allow you to produce a flat, or "tam-shaped," tam. You can make flat tams with wheel patterns which have more or fewer segments than seven, or with the yoke-type decreases which are described later, if you follow three simple principles.

1. Use a *maximum number of stitches* which is evenly divisible by the *number of decrease points*. (In other words, the number of stitches after all the increases have been made must be an even multiple of the number

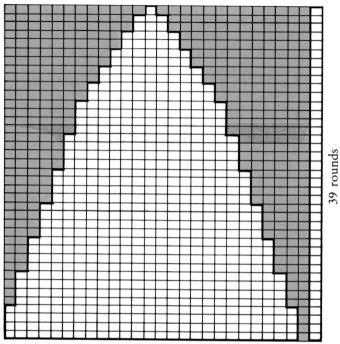

39 rounds

26 stitches per segment

Once you've figured the math for a revised tam, you can make a graph on which to plan color patterns. This one, taken from the example on pages 59–63, contains 39 rounds and 26 stitches in each segment. Decreases occur every fourth row for the first 26 rows, and then every second row for 13 rows. As you can see, a little fudging is required to make the graph, but the pattern of decreases is logical.

of decrease points.) In addition, *each* section of the tam must contain an odd number of stitches, plus one stitch for the decrease point.

2. Remember that using a different number of decrease points, a different rate of decrease, and/or a different maximum number of stitches will change the *number of rounds* needed to reach the center. When the number of rounds changes, the diameter of the wheel pattern changes.

3. Use the *8-stitch rule:* more than an average of 8 decreases in each round will make the hat ruffle. Including fewer than 8 decreases per round will cause less trouble, but will increase the number of rounds needed to reach the center—again, the diameter of the wheel pattern changes. If you want your tam to lie perfectly flat, keep the average rate of decreasing as close to 8 stitches per round as possible.

Plan the number of decrease points and the rate of decrease in the wheel pattern carefully. Then determine the wheel pattern diameter, and finally figure out how long the body of the tam will be. When you have these numbers, you will be able to figure the number of rounds available for border patterns and wheel patterns.

Altering the arrangement of decreases: other numbers of decrease points

To examine the idea of modification further, we will plan a tam with nine decrease points. Again, we will assume a desired diameter of 10 inches, and will make only the essential changes in the basic pattern. Several rates of decrease will be explored. They will affect the wheel pattern diameter and the body length.

D (hat diameter) = 10 inches
B (brim diameter) = 8.3 inches
W (wheel pattern diameter) = ?
L (body length) = ?

Once again, you can work these problems out on graph paper instead of going through all the math. As was explained for the alternative sequence of decreases (page 60), the answer you get from the graphing technique will be one row less than the answer from the math technique.

For a nine-point decrease, we want a maximum number of stitches which is an even number and divisible by 9. In this case, 180 stitches is evenly divisible by 9. Nine of these stitches will mark the decrease points.

180 − 9 = 171 stitches to use in 9 sections

$$\frac{171}{9} = 19 \text{ stitches per section}$$

(1) If we use the basic decrease pattern, with double decreases worked on every other row, we will remove 18 stitches on each decrease round (2 stitches each at 9 decrease points), for an average rate of decrease of 9 stitches per round:

$$\frac{\text{number of stitches decreased}}{\text{number of rounds over which decreasing occurs}} = \text{average rate of decrease}$$

$$\frac{18 \text{ stitches}}{2 \text{ rounds}} = 9 \text{ stitches/round}$$

The 8-stitch rule warns us that at this rate of decreasing the hat will ruffle. We need a ratio close to, but not over, an average of 8 decreases per round. Let's look at the possibilities.

(2) If we place two plain rounds after each decrease round, we will decrease 18 stitches every three rounds.

$$\frac{18 \text{ stitches}}{3 \text{ rounds}} = 6 \text{ stitches/round}$$

Our average rate of decrease is 6 stitches per round. If we eliminate 6 stitches per round, it will take us 180 / 6 or 30 rounds to complete the center wheel pattern.

Since we have changed the size of the wheel pattern, we need to refigure the tam to get a new body length. For the radius of the wheel pattern, 30 rounds divided by 11 rows per inch is 2.7 inches. The diameter is twice that, or 5.4 inches. Now we can use the usual formulas.

$$\frac{D - W}{2} = L \text{ above crease}$$

$$\frac{10 - 5.4}{2} = \frac{4.6}{2} = 2.3$$

$$\frac{D - B}{2} = L \text{ below crease}$$

$$\frac{10 - 8.3}{2} = \frac{1.7}{2} = .85$$

$$L \text{ above crease} + L \text{ below crease} + L$$
$$2.3 + .85 = 3.15$$

The graph shows this new wheel pattern.

(3) Next, let's work three rounds after each decrease round until half the stitches are gone, then return to using one plain round after each decrease round.

The first average rate of decrease:

$$\frac{18 \text{ stitches}}{4 \text{ rounds}} = 4.5 \text{ stitches/round}$$

We will reduce the first 90 stitches at this rate:

$$\frac{90}{4.5} = 20 \text{ rounds}$$

and it will take 20 rounds to accomplish this.

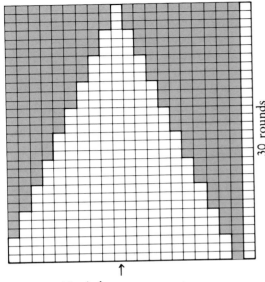

30 rounds

↑

20 stitches per segment

This is the graph for nine decrease points, with two plain rounds worked after each decrease round (the second example for other numbers of decrease points).

The second average rate of decrease:

$$\frac{18 \text{ stitches}}{2 \text{ rounds}} = 9 \text{ stitches/round}$$

We will reduce the final 90 stitches at this rate:

$$\frac{90}{9} = 10 \text{ rounds}$$

and it will take 10 rounds to accomplish this.

The entire pattern of decreases will require

$$20 + 10 = 30 \text{ rounds}$$

What about ruffling? The first average rate is low, but the second is high. We can figure the average rate of decrease for the entire wheel by adding together both rates of decrease, and dividing by 2 (because each is used for only half the stitches):

$$\frac{4.5 + 9}{2} = \frac{13.5}{2} = 6.75 \text{ overall rate of decrease}$$

The overall rate of decrease is lower than our 8-stitch goal, so there will be some extra fullness in the top of this tam.

Because this example requires 30 rounds to complete, as did the previous one, the diameter of the wheel and length of the body will be the same. However, the graph will look different because we have changed the placement of the decreases.

(4) Okay. Now let's work two plain rounds after each decrease round until half the stitches are gone, then return to using one plain round after each decrease round.

The first average rate of decrease:

$$\frac{18 \text{ stitches}}{3 \text{ rounds}} = 6 \text{ stitches/round}$$

We will reduce the first 90 stitches at this rate:

$$\frac{90}{6} = 15 \text{ rounds}$$

and it will take 15 rounds to accomplish this.

The second average rate of decrease:

$$\frac{18 \text{ stitches}}{2 \text{ rounds}} = 9 \text{ stitches/round}$$

We will reduce the final 90 stitches at this rate:

$$\frac{90}{9} = 10 \text{ rounds}$$

and it will take 10 rounds to accomplish this.

The entire pattern of decreases will require 15 + 10 = 25

$$15 + 10 = 25 \text{ rounds}$$

The average rate of decrease for the entire wheel is again figured by adding together both rates of decrease, and dividing by 2 (because each is used for only half the stitches):

$$\frac{6 + 9}{2} = \frac{15}{2} = 7.5 \text{ overall rate of decrease}$$

This is an average which is very close to the 8-stitch ideal.

For the radius of the wheel pattern, 25 rounds divided by 11 rows

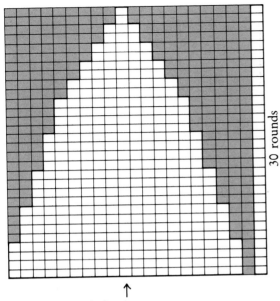

30 rounds

↑

20 stitches per segment

Again we have nine decrease points. Now half the stitches are eliminated with three plain rounds following each decrease round, and half are eliminated with one plain round following each decrease round (the third example).

per inch is 2.4 inches; the diameter, twice the radius, is 4.8 inches. Back to our formulas:

$$\frac{D - W}{2} = L \text{ above crease}$$

$$\frac{10 - 4.8}{2} = \frac{5.2}{2} = 2.6$$

$$\frac{D - B}{2} = L \text{ below crease}$$

$$\frac{10 - 8.3}{2} = \frac{1.7}{2} = .85$$

L above crease + L below crease + L
2.6 + .85 = 3.45

The new body length, 3.45, is very close to the original body length (3.5) and the graph will be like the one shown on page 70.

(5) Now let's analyze what we have found. All of the methods described above follow the 8-stitch rule: the results do not exceed an overall average of 8 decreases per round. All are workable if you adjust the

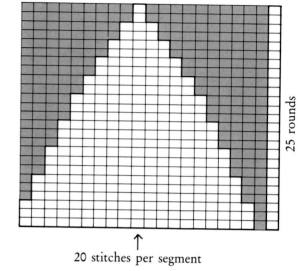

Nine decrease points, half the stitches eliminated with two plain rounds following each decrease round, and half with one plain round following each decrease round (the fourth example).

25 rounds

↑
20 stitches per segment

length of the body to suit the changes in the diameter of the wheel pattern.

If any method can be chosen as most appropriate, then method (4) requires the least amount of change in the basic pattern. It most closely approximates the basic pattern without exceeding the 8-stitch rule. The wheel pattern will take about 25 rows to complete and the body will only need to be adjusted by one or two rounds.

GARLAND PATTERNS AND YOKE-TYPE DECREASING

Sometimes you will need to solve special problems to make special tams. The flower garland shapes in "Grandma's Garden" are actually border-type patterns which I wanted to carry into the top of the tam. I needed to invent a way to place the decreases so they wouldn't interfere with the pattern.

I followed the basic pattern until I reached the point where the wheel pattern began. Then, in order to keep the patterns intact, I worked the pattern rounds without any decreases. Between garlands, however, I had to include all the decreases that should have occurred while I was knitting flowers.

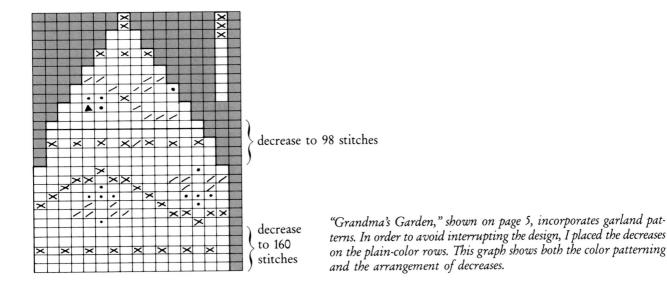

decrease to 98 stitches

decrease to 160 stitches

"Grandma's Garden," shown on page 5, incorporates garland patterns. In order to avoid interrupting the design, I placed the decreases on the plain-color rows. This graph shows both the color patterning and the arrangement of decreases.

At the point where the wheel pattern began, I worked one more garland pattern. I kept track of the decrease rounds which I was "skipping." The next normal decrease round was to occur two plain rounds after the garland, and it would need to contain its own decreases *plus* those of the rows I had "skipped." When you alter patterns like this, it's best to plan that your decreases will occur on a plain round which has at least one plain round on either side of it.

I was working with the concept of the basic tam, with its seven-point double decreases, and so wanted to maintain an average rate of decrease of 7 stitches per round. To determine the number of stitches I needed to decrease on my first actual decrease round, I added the number of rounds of the border pattern and the two plain rows, then multiplied by the average decrease rate of 7.

I repeated this process after the next border pattern, then began a small wheel pattern on the remaining stitches. (See the section on border patterns for other garland borders.)

Again, I was dealing with challenges both of shaping and of color patterning. The garland patterns are lovely, but they are difficult to knit because you must carry more than two colors—sometimes as many as five—at once. Because these designs require long yarn carries, you must remember to weave in the yarns. I don't recommend that you try a garland pattern for your first venture into color-pattern knitting, unless you stick to two colors.

However, you may want to warm up by experimenting with this type of shaping and using a simpler type of border pattern on the top of your tam.

The graph shows the entire pattern of "Grandma's Garden" from the first decrease point.

WALL TAMS

Wall tams are wheel patterns made to fit stretchers or hoops. A wall tam is usually larger than a hat, and it presents its own planning problems. The size of a wall tam is determined by the diameter of the hoop or stretcher on which it will be displayed; for the examples here, we'll assume you have a 15-inch hoop.

You'll be knitting just the "top" of the tam, plus enough of the bottom (a ribbing or casing) to hold it in place on its mounting. Because the tam has to be large enough to cover the stretcher, the circumference of the stretcher is an essential number in your calculations. It determines the maximum number of stitches in the wall tam.

circumference = diameter × 3.14 (*or* π)
  for example, 15 × 3.14 = 47.1 inches
frame diameter = _____ inches
frame circumference = _____ inches

Once you have these dimensions and your stitch and row gauge, you can determine the number of stitches which will be required to fit your stretcher:

frame circumference × stitch gauge = maximum number of stitches in tam

Choose the number of decrease points that you want in your tam and make sure your maximum number of stitches is divisible by the number of decrease points. For the example here, I will use the arrangement which worked best for "other numbers of decrease points" on the smaller tam (number 4): there will be nine decrease points, half the stitches will be decreased with two plain rounds following each decrease round, and half the stitches will be decreased with one plain round following each decrease round.

Two wall tams: the larger format permits exploration of more intricate patterns.

There are three ways to go at the problem of making large circular forms, or "wall tams."

(1) The simplest method of constructing a wall tam is to work from the *center out*, increasing evenly until you reach your maximum number of stitches. As in the regular tams, the rate of increase will affect the diameter of the wheel.

(2) If you work from the outside in, as usual, graph paper can again do the trick for those who are visually inclined. Make an appropriate graph, based on the maximum number of stitches, the number of wheel segments, and the desired rate of decrease. Then count rows for the wheel pattern and divide by the row gauge to get the wheel radius. Multiply by 2 to get the wheel pattern diameter. Go to the formula for the top of the tam to get the needed body length:

$$\frac{D - W}{2} = L \text{ above crease}$$

You will not need to work the body below the crease.

(3) Again, you can choose to explore the mathematical nature of tams. At a gauge of 7 stitches and 11 rows per inch, we'll plan a tam to fit the 15-inch frame.

circumference × stitch gauge = maximum number of stitches in tam
$$47 \times 7 = 329$$

For nine decrease points, we need a number close to this which is divisible by 9. We can divide 329 by 9 to discover how close we are:

$$\frac{329}{9} = 36.5$$

To get an even number of stitches divisible by 9, we round off:

$$36 \times 9 = 324$$

To begin the tam, we can either work a casing and insert elastic, or use ribbing as in the regular tam. For the latter, use the smaller size of needles and cast on 80% of your maximum number:

$$324 \times .80 = 260$$

Work one inch of ribbing, which will help hold the tam on the frame. Increase to the maximum number of stitches.

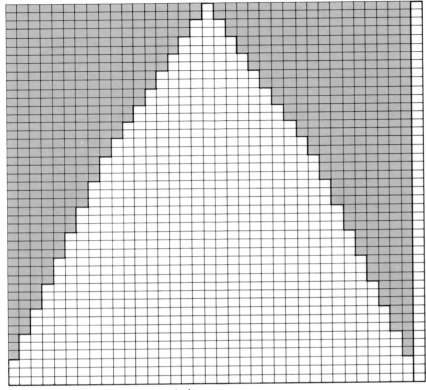

36 stitches per segment

Graph showing arrangement of decreases for a wall tam with nine decrease points and two rates of decreasing, as described in the text.

You now need to figure the diameter of the wheel pattern as before, and there are two rates of decrease:

$$\frac{18 \text{ stitches}}{3 \text{ rounds}} = 6 \text{ stitches/round}$$

$$\frac{18 \text{ stitches}}{2 \text{ rounds}} = 9 \text{ stitches/round}$$

A total of 324 stitches are being decreased, 162 at the first rate and 162 at the second rate:

$$\frac{162 \text{ stitches}}{6 \text{ stitches/round}} = 27 \text{ rounds}$$

$$\frac{162 \text{ stitches}}{9 \text{ stitches/round}} = 18 \text{ rounds}$$

So the wheel pattern will require:

27 + 18 = 45 rounds

Divide the number of rounds by the row gauge to get the radius of the wheel pattern, and then its diameter:

$$\frac{45}{11} = 4.15 \text{ inches} \times 2 = 8.3 \text{ inches}$$

Return to the usual formula for the top of a tam to determine the length to knit between the ribbing and the beginning of the wheel pattern:

$$\frac{D - W}{2} = L \text{ above crease}$$

$$\frac{15 - 8.3}{2} = \frac{6.7}{2} = 3.35 \text{ inches}$$

TAM MASTERY

Once you've reached this point, you can knit a tam for anyone, with any number of decreases, and with infinite varieties of patterns. Should you sail into the uncharted seas of other types of decreases and shaping, let me know how your experiments work out.

PART 7
Summary

When you plan your first tams, the following principles will help make your knitting more pleasant and certainly easier. Once you understand the principles thoroughly, you can break the bounds of their limitations and create new applications and extensions.

1. *Knit with only two colors at one time.*
2. *Carry unused colors no more than 1 inch.*
3. *Keep the same level of contrast between foreground and background colors.*
4. *Practice the 8-stitch rule.*

THE ESSENTIAL TAM

A tam, reduced to its essence, consists of the following parts:

1 inch of ribbing
23–44 rounds of border pattern (this is the *body*), consisting of:
   3–5 plain rounds of background color
   11–15 rounds of a border pattern
   3–5 plain rounds of background color
   3–7 rounds of a second border
   3–5 plain rounds of background color
about 26 rounds of wheel patterning

TAM WORKSHEET
Yarn

Work a gauge sample and determine both stitch and row gauges for your yarn. The ribbing will be worked on needles one or two sizes smaller than those used for the body of the hat.

Stitches/inch   = _____
Rows/inch   = _____
Body needle size   = _____
Ribbing needle size = _____

Finished diameter of tam and number of decrease points

Decide how many inches across you want the finished tam to be, and how many decrease points you want to use in the top.

finished diameter of tam (D) = _____ inches
number of decrease points   = _____

Ribbing

Measure the head size around the ears. Multiply this measurement by the stitch gauge to get the number of stitches in the full circumference of the head.

head size (around ears) = _____
                        × _____ stitches/inch
                        = _____ stitches in full circumference

Because ribbing is elastic, you will cast on approximately 80% of this number of stitches.

number of stitches × .80 = _____ stitches to cast on for ribbing

The final number of stitches in the ribbing needs to be divisible by 2 (for k1, p1 ribbing) or by 4 (for k2, p2 ribbing).

adjusted number of stitches to cast on = _____

Body

The body of the tam is the distance above the ribbing to the beginning of the decreases for the top. It is worked on the maximum number of stitches in the tam, and all increases occur immediately following the ribbing. See pages 29–31 for things to consider when deciding how much to increase for the body. If you plan to use color border patterns in the body (pages 84–90), be sure that the number of stitches in the body can accommodate the pattern repeats. (See the "fudge factor," pages 23–24.)

number of stitches in ribbing = _____
percentage of increase = _____
number of stitches after increase = _____

Adjust this number so it is evenly divisible by the number of decrease points you will use for the top of the tam.

maximum number of stitches in tam = _____

Divide the maximum number of stitches by the stitch gauge to get what we call the brim circumference (C). Divide that number by 3.14 to arrive at the brim diameter (B), which will be used in later calculations.

$$\frac{\text{maximum number of stitches in tam}}{\text{stitches/inch}} = C \div 3.14 = B$$

B = _____

You will determine the length of the body after designing the top or wheel.

Top or wheel

If you work with the seven-point double decreases, the number of rounds needed to complete the decrease area of the top, or the wheel, will be roughly equal to the number of stitches around the body of the tam divided by the number of decrease points. In other words, each wheel segment will have about the same number of rows as stitches. To develop precise numbers which apply to any arrangement of decreases, see the information on pages 59–70. If you are using a color pattern in the top, design your own or see the graphs for wheel patterns on pages 91–95.

number of rounds in top or wheel = _____

Determine also the diameter of the wheel or top decrease area (W) as follows:

$$\frac{\text{number of rounds}}{\text{row gauge}} \times 2 = W$$

W = _____

Length of body

The length of the body (L) is determined through the use of the formulas on pages 57 and 58, summarized here:

$$\frac{D - W}{2} = \text{L above crease}$$

$$\frac{D - B}{2} = \text{L below crease}$$

L above crease + L below crease = L

L = _____

Knitting and finishing

Work ribbing for 1 inch. Increase to maximum number of stitches, and work body to the length figured above (including color patterns, if desired). Begin top decrease area (and color wheel pattern, if desired). When 14 stitches remain, *k1, k2tog* (or use appropriate finish for optional decrease methods, pages 54–56). Check finishing options, page 53, or draw yarn through loops, gather up, and pull yarn to the center and secure it. Block.

The blank graph here is planned for the use of a seven-point decrease on the top of the tam, using double decreases on every other round. The graph shown is for 7 stitches and 11 rows per inch, and 26 rows are required to complete the top decreases. You can use 24 rows (counting from the top) to design a tam at 6 stitches per inch, or 20 rows for a tam at 5 stitches per inch.

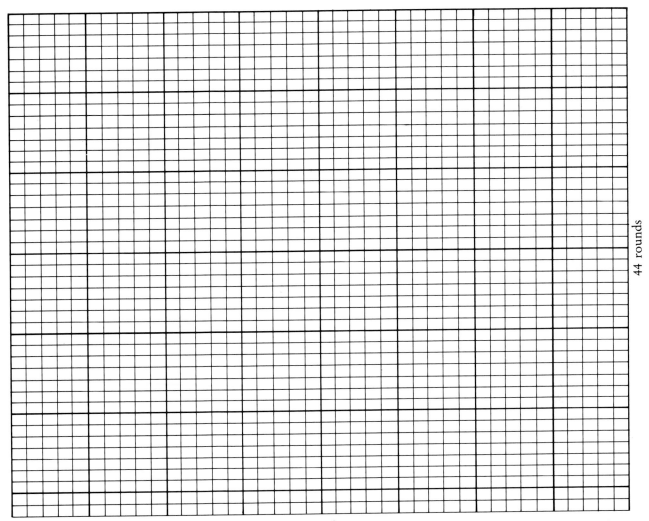

44 rounds

30 stitches

Blank graph for planning border pattern sequences. This graph is wide enough to accommodate designs for all weights of yarns.

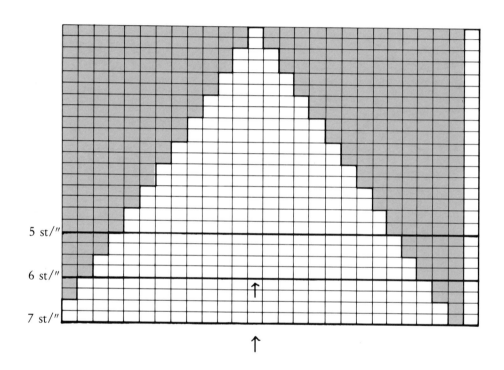

5 st/"

6 st/"

7 st/"

Blank graph for planning wheel segment patterns. This graph is set up for use with double decreases every two rounds, and can be adapted for use with three weights of yarn.

Afterword

The world of circular design forms—mandalas, wheel patterns, and, finally, tams—can be infinitely intriguing. Just as the teleidoscope infinitely reflects the world around you, so can your wheel pattern reflect your world, your ideas, and yourself without bounds. This type of knitting is both introspective and reflective. In a number of cultures, the circular mandala has served as a tool for meditation and spiritual development. Perhaps the wheel patterns we create can carry the same spiritual harmony. Whatever your philosophy, I think you will find them endlessly fascinating. Enjoy.

—Mary Rowe

The world is your kaleidoscope and the varying combinations of colors which it presents to you at every succeeding moment are the exquisitely adjusted images of your ever moving thoughts.

James Allen

Appendix

BORDER PATTERNS
Repeats are marked with brackets.

Group A
9- to 17-round OXO-pattern borders.

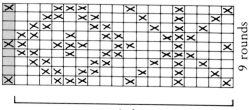

9 rounds

18 stitches

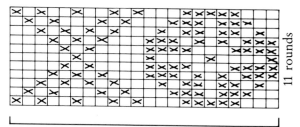

11 rounds

22 stitches

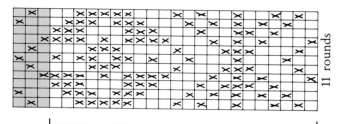

11 rounds

22 stitches

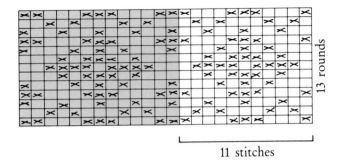

11 stitches

13 rounds

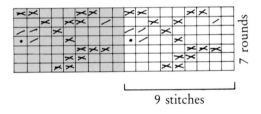

12 stitches

9 rounds

7- to 9-round garland pattern borders (require more than two colors per round).

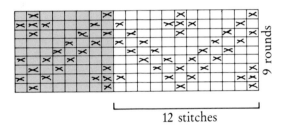

9 stitches

7 rounds

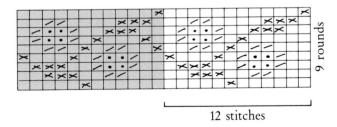

12 stitches

9 rounds

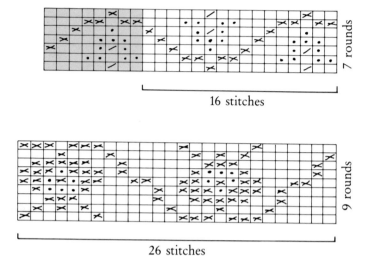

7 rounds

16 stitches

9 rounds

26 stitches

WHEEL PATTERNS

These graphs are planned for use with the basic tam's decrease sequence, using seven segments and double decreases on every other round. They are designed for 26-stitch segments and, with one exception which is marked, for 26 rounds.

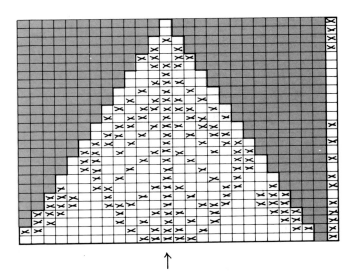

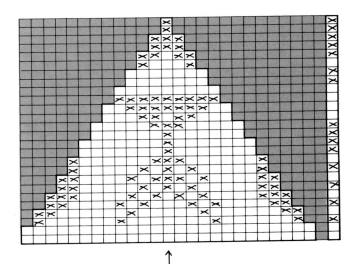

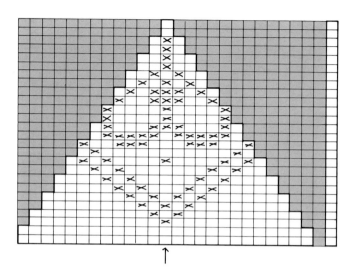

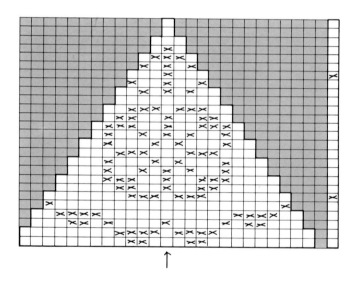

1	white
1a	natural/cream
3	beige
4	moorit (brown)
5	natural black
15	sky blue
19	lavender
23	yellow/light yellow heather
29	green lovat
32	pumpkin
33	tartan blue (used with reds)
38	burnt orange heather
55	garnet
72	strawberry
82	loden
129	coral
203	silver/grey
1293	dragonfly
FC15	sky blue
FC22	lavender pink
FC24	light green heather
FC34	robin's egg
FC43	honey beige
FC47	bressay blue
FC48	navy
FC49	tartan blue (used with lavenders)
FC50	smoky pink
FC54	lavender heather
FC56	plum
FC57	light brown heather
FC58	brown heather

Source List

Yarn Manufacturers

Brown Sheep Top of the Lamb
Brown Sheep Co.
10062 Cty. Rd. 16
Mitchell, NE 69357
www.brownsheep.com

Jamieson and Smith
90 N. Road
Lerwick, Shetland Isles ZE1 0PQ
Scotland
www.shetland-wool-
brokers.zetnet.co.uk
Shetland yarn

Plymouth Yarn Co.
500 Lafayette St.
Bristol, PA 19007
www.plymouthyarn.com
Alpaca yarn

Reynolds Yarn
35 Scales Ln.
Townsend, MA 01469-1094
Alpaca yarn

Sources for Jamieson and Smith Shetland yarn in the United States

Blue Hill Yarn Shop
Rte. 172
Blue Hill, ME 04614

Colorful Stitches
PO Box 2278
Lenox, MA 01240
www.colorful-stitches.com

The Elegant Ewe
71 S. Main St.
Concord, NH 03301
www.elegantewe.com

The Handworks Gallery
2911 Kavanaugh Blvd.
Little Rock, AR 72205
www.handworksgallery.com

Knitting Basket
2054 Mountain Blvd.
Oakland, CA 94610
www.theknittingbasket.com

Needlepoint Joint
241 Historic 25th St.
Ogden, UT 84401
www.needlepointjoint.com

Schoolhouse Press
6899 Cary Bluff Rd.
Pittsville, WI 54466
www.schoolhousepress.com

Simply Shetland
PO Box 751264
Petaluma, CA 94975-1264
www.simplyshetland.net

Uncommon Threads
293 State St.
Los Altos, CA 94022
www.uncommonthreadsyarn.com

Webs
75 Service Center Rd.
Northampton, MA 01061
www.yarn.com

Woodland Woolworks
PO Box 850
Carlton, OR 97111
www.woodlandwoolworks.com

The Wool Connection
34 E. Main St.
Avon, CT 06001
www.woolconnection.com

Wooly West
PO Box 58306
Salt Lake City, UT 84158
www.woolywest.com

The Yarn Barn
24 Seldon St.
Woodbridge, CT 06525
www.theyarnbarn.com

Yarn Barn of Andersonville
5077 Andersonville Rd.
Dillwyn, VA 23936
www.yarnbarn.com

Yarn Barn of Kansas
930 Massachusetts
Lawrence, KS 66044
www.yarnbarn-ks.com

Bibliography

*Indicates the most useful materials.

Baker, Cozy. *Through the Kaleidoscope and Beyond. . . .* Annapolis, Maryland: Beechcliff Books, 1987. Contains information about designers, types of scopes, sources, and lovely pictures of kaleidoscope interiors. Available from the Brewster Society, 100 Severn Avenue, Suite 605, Annapolis, Maryland 21403; phone (301) 263-3580.

Don, Sarah. *Fair Isle Knitting.* New York: St. Martin's Press, 1979. Graphed Fair Isle designs, along with sweater patterns and color notes.

Eischen, Joyce. *Parchment Silhouette Snowflakes.* Tree Toys, n.d. Interesting collections of snowflake designs printed on parchment to be folded, cut, and displayed. Excellent source for shapes or motifs to use on wheel pattern designs. Several different leaflets are available from Tree Toys, P.O. Box 492, Hinsdale, Illinois 60521.

Fassett, Kaffe. *Glorious Knits.* New York: Westminster Trading Corp., 1985. Explore this for an education in the uses of color.

Gottfridsson, Inger, and Ingrid Gottfridsson. *The Swedish Mitten Book.* Asheville, North Carolina: Lark Books, 1984. Lovely floral mitten patterns from Gotland are graphed and can be readily adapted to tams.

Harrell, Betsy. *Anatolian Knitting Designs.* Istanbul, Turkey: Redhouse Press, 1981. Pattern graphs from traditional Turkish socks.

*Knitter's graph paper. Schoolhouse Press, Pittsville, Wisconsin. This graph paper has the correct number of rows per inch in relation to the number of stitches per inch. This will allow your graphs to predict accurately what you will knit. Essential to the color-pattern knitter.

*McGregor, Sheila. *The Complete Book of Traditional Fair Isle Knitting.* New York: Charles Scribner's Sons, 1982. This wonderful book contains excellent historical notes on the development of Fair Isle knitting. The color notes are particularly interesting. The most useful section of the book is "Part 6: The Pattern Notebook." Pages of traditional Fair Isle patterns are graphed and grouped by type and by the number of rows needed to complete the pattern. An absolute must for the Fair Isle knitter.

Pearson, Michael. *Traditional Knitting*, London: Collins Publishing, 1984. (Distributed by Schoolhouse Press, Pittsville, Wisconsin.) The section called "Two-colored knitting of the Shetland Isles and Fair Isle" contains interesting pattern graphs and color notes. Of particular interest are the unusual color combinations in the sweaters by the Garrick sisters.

Rutt, Richard. *A History of Hand Knitting*. Loveland, Colorado: Interweave Press, 1988. Fascinating history of hand knitting in Europe. Extensively researched with pictures of knitted artifacts and intriguing knitting stories.

*Smith, Mary, and Maggie Twatt. *Shetland Pattern Book*. Shetland Times Ltd., 1979. Excellent source of traditional patterns from the pattern books of the authors and other local knitters.

Stanley, Montse. *The Handknitter's Handbook*. New York: Sterling Books, 1986. Everything you wanted to know about knitting techniques including several ways to do the tubular cast on for rib. Encyclopedic in nature. Hundreds of clear line drawings.

————. "Knitting a Perfect Rib." *Threads*, No. 15, February/March, 1988. More notes on cast ons and cast offs to use with ribbing. Excellent comments on various technical points of constructing the perfect rib.

Starmore, Alice. *Alice Starmore's Book of Fair Isle Knitting*. Newtown, Connecticut: Taunton Press, 1988. Excellent source on Fair Isle knitting with detailed notes on technique. Fascinating discussion on the development of the Fair Isle knitting traditions. A few notes on tam construction.

————. "Designing a Wheel Pattern Fair Isle Tammy." *Threads*, No. 20, December 1988/January 1989. Very good article on traditional shaping of wheel pattern tams. Excellent illustrations and diagrams.

————. "Fair Isle Knitting." *Threads*, No. 8, December/January 1987. Interesting article on traditional methods of stranded color knitting in the round. Note the tam on the cover.

Upitis, Lizbeth. *Latvian Mittens*. St. Paul, Minnesota: Dos Tejedoras, 1981. Unusual book written in both Latvian and English contains traditional designs and techniques used in the colorful Latvian mittens. Historical, literary, and social traditions connected with Latvian mittens are included. Graphs, color notes, and techniques are useful to the tam knitter in quest of color patterns.

*Zimmermann, Elizabeth. *Knitters Almanac*. New York: Dover, 1978. *Knitting Without Tears*, New York: Charles Scribner's Sons, 1971. *Knitting Workshop*. Pittsville, Wisconsin: Schoolhouse Press, 1986. "Elizabeth Zimmermann's Knitting Glossary" (video). Pittsville, Wisconsin: Schoolhouse Press, 1987. "Knitting Workshop" (video). Pittsville, Wisconsin: Schoolhouse Press, 1987.

These works present basic techniques in an entertaining way. They include Elizabeth Zimmermann's unusual philosophy of "thinking knitters' freedom from patterns" and her outstanding EPS (Elizabeth's Percentage System), which liberates you to design in *any* size. (Any size is correct, I tested it!)

*————, and Meg Swansen. *Wool Gathering*, semiannual knitting newsletter produced by Elizabeth Zimmermann and Meg Swansen. Available for $1.50 each or by subscription of 6 issues (3 years for $7.50). These contain Elizabeth and Meg's nifty designs and techniques. Included in each issue are descriptions of new books on the knitting scene. Some issues have been reproduced under a new name: *Spun Out #8* (old *Wool Gathering* issues #20, March 1979, and #21, September 1979) contains the first patterned tams I ever saw. See the source list for the address and be sure to ask for Meg's book list—it's a real treat!

Index

Knitted Tams, Index, Galley 1, Revised 8-25-89

A History of Hand Knitting 2
abbreviations 17–18
Alice Starmore's Book of Fair Isle Knitting
  3, 11
anatomy of the tam 27
average rate of decrease per row 60–61

basic tam 6, 19–24, 35, 77
beret 2, 6
blocking 21–22
body length 28, 32–33, 57–63, 65, 80
body of the tam 20, 28, 57–59
border patterns 7, 84–90
brim 27
brim circumference 27, 30, 79
brim diameter 27, 32, 57, 60, 65, 79
button center finish 53

carrying yarn 11–12, 72
center finishes 53
circular design 1
circumference of brim 29, 30, 79
circumference/diameter conversion 72
clockwise swirl top decrease 54
color numbers for Shetland yarn 96–97
color selection 8, 44–51, 77
counterclockwise swirl top decrease 55
crease 27–31, 57–59, 62–63

decreases 17, 20, 21, 54–56
diameter of brim 27, 32, 57, 60, 65, 79
diameter of finished tam 26–27, 32, 60,
  65
diameter of wheel pattern 28, 32, 57–63,
  65, 79
diameter/circumference conversion 72
double decrease 17, 20, 21
duplicate stitching 8, 12

eight-stitch rule 64, 69–70, 77
elastic cord 10
equipment 10
essential tam 77

Fair Isle patterns 1, 3, 11, 45–46
fiber selection 7–8
finishes 21, 53
floral edge 40
fudge factor 23–24, 79

garland patterns 70–72
gauge 28–29, 78
graphed patterns 13–15, 23, 37–42, 61,
  64, 67, 70, 71
graphs, how to read 12

heptagon 37

increase at brim 29–30
increase, raised bar 18

kaleidoscopes 1–2, 83
knitter's graph paper 10
Knitting Workshop 1

leaf pattern 41
length of body 28, 32–33, 57–63, 65, 80
length of wheel segment (*also see* wheel
  radius) 28
loop center finish 53

McGregor, Sheila 1

needles 10, 78

pattern area 28
Pearson, Michael 46
petal edge pattern 40
pompon center finish 53

rate of decrease 28, 60–70
ribbing 6, 16, 20, 21, 25–26, 27, 72, 78
Rutt, Richard 2, 3

scallop pattern 39
shaping a tam 6, 52–59
Shetland Islands 1, 2
Shetland jumper weight wool yarn 7
Shetland yarn color numbers 96–97
sizing 25
Spun Out 1
star pattern 38
Starmore, Alice 3
stitch markers 10
stranded color pattern knitting 3, 11
stretcher 10, 72–76
Swansen, Meg vi
swatch 28–29, 78
Swiss embroidery 8, 12

tab center finish 53
The Complete Book of Fair Isle Knitting 1
tubular cast on 16

variation in color patterning 44–52, 63
variation in shape 52–59

wall tams 72–76
washing the tam 21
weaving in 12, 72
wheel area 28
wheel pattern diameter 28, 32, 57–63,
   65, 79
wheel pattern graphs 91–95
wheel pattern radius 62
wheel patterning 1, 6, 7, 35–43, 83
Wool Gathering 1
worksheet 78–82

yarn amounts needed 8
yarn selection 7
yarn sources 98–99
yoke-type decreasing 70–72

zigzag top decrease 56
Zimmermann, Elizabeth 1, 35